OECD ECONOMIC SURVEYS

1993-1994

GERMANY

ORGANISATION FOR ECONOMIC CO-OPERATION AND DEVELOPMENT

ORGANISATION FOR ECONOMIC CO-OPERATION AND DEVELOPMENT

Pursuant to Article 1 of the Convention signed in Paris on 14th December 1960, and which came into force on 30th September 1961, the Organisation for Economic Co-operation and Development (OECD) shall promote policies designed:

— to achieve the highest sustainable economic growth and employment and a rising standard of living in Member countries, while maintaining financial stability, and thus to contribute to the development of the world economy;

— to contribute to sound economic expansion in Member as well as non-member countries in the process of economic development; and

— to contribute to the expansion of world trade on a multilateral, non-discriminatory basis in accordance with international obligations.

The original Member countries of the OECD are Austria, Belgium, Canada, Denmark, France, Germany, Greece, Iceland, Ireland, Italy, Luxembourg, the Netherlands, Norway, Portugal, Spain, Sweden, Switzerland, Turkey, the United Kingdom and the United States. The following countries became Members subsequently through accession at the dates indicated hereafter: Japan (28th April 1964), Finland (28th January 1969), Australia (7th June 1971), New Zealand (29th May 1973) and Mexico (18th May 1994). The Commission of the European Communities takes part in the work of the OECD (Article 13 of the OECD Convention).

Publié également en français.

Table of contents

Box

Tables

Diagrams

BASIC STATISTICS OF GERMANY

THE LAND

		Major cities, June 1991	Thousand inhabitants
Area, 1992 (thousand sq. km)	356.7		
Agricultural area, 1991 (thousand sq. km)	191.8		
Forests, 1992 (thousand sq. km)	95.2	Berlin	3 438
		Hamburg	1 661
		Munich	1 237
		Cologne	956
		Frankfurt	647
		Essen	626
		Dortmund	600
		Stuttgart	584
		Düsseldorf	577
		Bremen	552

THE PEOPLE

Population (thousands), 1992	80 975	Labour force total (thousand), 1993[1]	30 922
Number of inhabitants per sq. km	227	Civilian employment (thousand), 1993[1]	29 014
Net natural increase in population, 1992	-76 329	*of which:* Agriculture	880
Net migration (thousands), 1992	+788	Industry	10 823
		Other activities	17 311

PRODUCTION

GDP, 1993 (billions of DM)	3 107	Origin of GDP, 1993 (per cent):	
GDP per head, 1993 (US$)	23 217	Agriculture, forestry, fishing	1.1
Gross fixed investment (1993):		Industry (incl. construction)	35.3
per cent of GDP	22.7	Services	63.6
per head (US$)	5 273		

THE GOVERNMENT

			Seats
Public consumption, 1993 (per cent of GDP)	20.0	Composition of Federal Parliament:	
General government current revenue,		Social Democrats (SPD)	239
1993 (per cent of GDP)	47.9	Christian Democrats (CDU)	267
Public debt end 1993 (ratio to		Free Democrats (FDP)	78
general government current revenue)	96.5	Christian Socialists (CSU)	50
		PDS	15
		B90/Greens	7
		Independents	6
		Last general election: 02.12.1990	
		Next general election: October 1994	

FOREIGN TRADE

Exports:		Imports:	
Exports of goods and services		Imports of goods and services	
as per cent of GDP, 1992	23.7	as per cent of GDP, 1992	23.9
Main exports, 1992 (per cent		Main imports, 1992 (per cent	
of total merchandise exports):		of total merchandise imports):	
Products of agriculture,		Food	11
forestry and fishing	1	Raw materials and semi-finished goods	15
Basic materials and semi-finished goods	23	Finished goods	73
Manufactured foods and tobacco	5	*of which:*	
Other consumer manufactures	13	Primary products	13
Investment goods	57	End products	60
Other exports	1	Other imports	1
Total	100	Total	100

THE CURRENCY

Monetary unit: Deutschemark		Currency units per US$, average of	
		daily figures:	
		Year 1993	1.653
		June 1994	1.629

1. Excluding eastern Germany.
Note: An international comparison of certain basic statistics is given in an annex table.

This Survey is based on the Secretariat's study prepared for the annual review of Germany by the Economic and Development Review Committee on 27th June 1994.

•

After revisions in the light of discussions during the review, final approval of the Survey for publication was given by the Committee on 27th July 1994.

•

The previous Survey of Germany was issued in August 1993.

Introduction

Following the sharp fall in GDP in late 1992 and the first quarter of 1993, there are clear signs that a recovery is under way, based mainly on a rebound in exports, housing investment, and buoyant activity in eastern Germany. In the western part of the country, personal consumption continues to be restrained by high unemployment and falling real household income, while business fixed investment remains weak, despite lower interest rates. Growth in 1994 is expected to be moderate, especially since fiscal restraint is likely to have a negative short-term demand impact. The recovery should, however, gradually gather pace as better profitability leads to higher business investment, a stabilisation of the labour market and stronger consumer confidence, as the beneficial effects of fiscal retrenchment on confidence feed through to the business sector and as further progress is made in the reconstruction of the eastern German economy. Greater price stability has allowed policy-controlled interest rates to fall, thereby supporting the recovery.

Looking further ahead, medium-term growth prospects depend quite critically on a sustained improvement in German competitiveness, which has deteriorated over the last few years. The reasons for the deterioration are complex and insofar as they are cyclical in nature are being partially corrected through current wage moderation. More fundamentally, however, they may also relate to structural defects in the economy which were covered up by the unification boom but which have now been unmasked by recession. In particular, the problem of excessive costs can be traced not just to excess demand for labour during the boom, but to high taxes and heavy social charges, wage rigidities and over-regulation. Moreover, though the principle of the "social market economy" continues to generate a high degree of social consensus, a recent federal government report has expressed concern that an excessive concentration on distributional objectives may have led to a diminished ability to respond to adjustments in the international division of labour. Complicated bureaucratic procedures may have impeded technological innovation. Employment creation may be being compromised by impediments to expansion and competition in the service-producing sector, the opportunities of which Germany has been slow to exploit because of an over-concentration on its traditional areas of strength in manufacturing industry.

Part I of the *Survey* reviews the evidence for an economic recovery being underway and assesses the degree of convergence between the east and west German economies, together with the short-term outlook and the risks attached to it. Part II describes the evolution of monetary policy over the review period and discusses the monetary stance. The fiscal consolidation programme is analysed in Part III, from a medium-term perspective. The special chapter of the *Survey* (Part IV) examines the arguments, noted above, that many of Germany's current problems have their origin in structural rigidities which may harm its medium-term growth prospects – the motivation for a programme of supply-side measures, including deregulation and privatisation, being undertaken by the government. Part V presents the Conclusions.

I. Overcoming the recession – Recent macroeconomic developments

Stabilisation of activity in the west

How firmly based is the recovery?

The fall in demand and output in western Germany, which had started in spring 1992 and accelerated sharply around the turn of 1992/93, came to a halt in early 1993, as both exports and domestic demand stabilised and even rebounded somewhat later in the year (Diagram 1). Hence, while for the whole of 1993 GDP fell by 1.9 per cent, it rose by a seasonally adjusted ½ per cent in the second

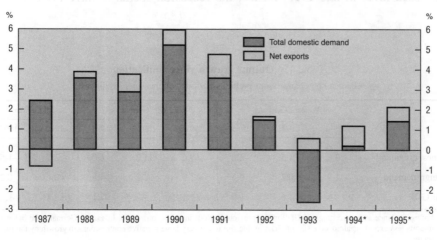

Diagram 1. **DOMESTIC DEMAND AND NET EXPORTS IN WESTERN GERMANY**
Contribution to GDP growth (percentage points)

* Projections.
Source: OECD.

quarter and by a further 1 per cent in the third, before relapsing ½ per cent towards year-end.[1] While the annual decline was the strongest in post-war history, exceeding the one in the wake of the first oil price shock, the output gap which appeared was relatively less severe given the previous over-utilisation of capacity due to the reunification boom (Tables 1 and 2).

The extent of the 1993 slump in activity was not only somewhat milder than expected but its profile also differed somewhat from what had been foreseen. Thus, the fall early in the year was distinctly more pronounced, while the rebound was initially unexpectedly strong before weakening again in the last quarter. The reasons for this bumpy profile of recession and recovery are that, on the one hand, the fall in exports was quite steep but short-lived, while, on the other, domestic private households have been slow and somewhat erratic in adapting to their more constrained circumstances and in their reaction to policy decisions which affected expected incomes.

Following the fall in GDP in the fourth quarter of 1993, a rebound of activity occurred early in 1994. Exports continued their upward trend, even though some major markets in continental Europe remain sluggish. Domestic demand, while remaining relatively weak overall, does not appear to have declined further in 1994, as had been expected as a consequence of squeezed wages and cuts in social transfers. Retail sales even rose somewhat from their depressed level in late 1993. Hence, the recession seems to have bottomed out

Table 1. **Output growth since unification**

Percentage change from previous period; volumes in 1991 prices

	Western Germany			Eastern Germany			All Germany	
	1991	1992	1993	1991	1992	1993	1992	1993
Domestic demand	3.6	1.5	−2.6	9.6	11.2	6.0	2.7	−1.5
Foreign demand[1]	1.2	0.2	0.6	−42.9	−12.2	−4.8	−0.6	0.2
Real GDP	4.5	1.6	−1.9	−31.4	9.7	7.1	2.1	−1.3

1. Foreign balance as a percentage of GDP in the previous period; includes intra trade. In eastern Germany the balance of imports less exports is almost the size of GDP, giving rise to the very large negative contributions to growth by the foreign sector.

Source: Statistisches Bundesamt, Volkswirtschaftliche Gesamtrechnungen; and DIW, Wochenbericht, No. 13/93, Vol. 60, Berlin 1993.

Table 2. **Demand and output in western Germany**

	1991 current prices		1992	1993
	DM billion	Per cent of GDP	Percentage change (volume)	
Demand and output				
Government consumption	466.5	17.7	3.2	−1.3
Gross fixed investment	564.9	21.4	1.1	−6.9
Construction	302.1	11.5	5.5	−0.4
Machinery and equipment	262.8	10.0	−3.9	−15.0
Final domestic demand	2 459.7	93.3	1.8	−1.8
Stockbuilding[1]	6.6	0.3	−0.3	−0.7
Total domestic demand	2 466.3	93.6	1.5	−2.6
Exports of goods and services	892.5	33.9	3.7	−6.1
Imports of goods and services	723.9	27.5	3.9	−9.6
Foreign balance[1]	168.7	6.4	0.2	0.6
GDP at constant prices			**1.6**	**−1.9**
GDP at current prices	2 635.0	100.0	6.0	1.3
GDP price deflator			4.4	3.3

1. The yearly rates of change refer to changes expressed as a percentage of GDP in the previous year.
Source: Statistisches Bundesamt.

and given way to gradual recovery. This is confirmed by recent forward-looking indicators (Diagram 2). Orders in manufacturing rose strongly in the period February through May, exceeding their year-earlier level by more than 6 per cent. Capacity utilisation has passed the cyclical trough and business is regaining confidence, as shown by the Ifo climate indicator.

Rebound in exports

As had been signalled for some time by rising foreign orders in manufacturing, merchandise exports started picking up in mid-1993 from the low level to which they had fallen. Measured from the peak in the fourth quarter 1991 to the trough in the second quarter 1993, the decline (at current values) amounted to about 14 per cent. By the end of 1993, exports had made up nearly half of the fall, reaching roughly their year-earlier level. The upward trend has continued, as evidenced by the unabated rise in foreign orders and results from business surveys.

Diagram 2. CYCLICAL INDICATORS FOR WESTERN GERMANY

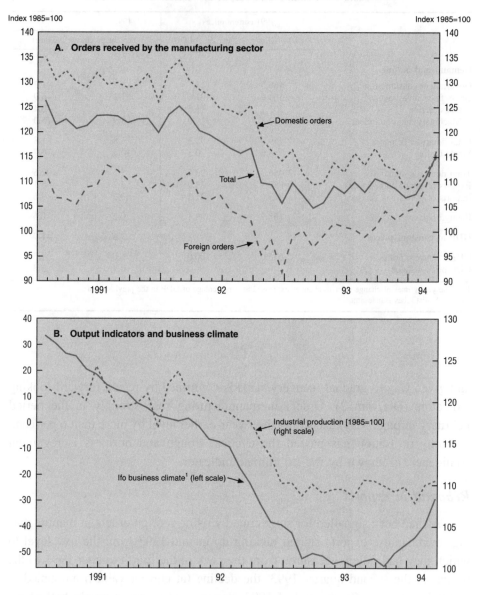

1. Difference between favorable and unfavorable responses to a survey on changes in short-term business outlook expressed in percent of total responses. A negative number indicates a majority of unfavorable responses.
Source: OECD, Ifo-Institut and Deutsche Bundesbank, *Monthly Report.*

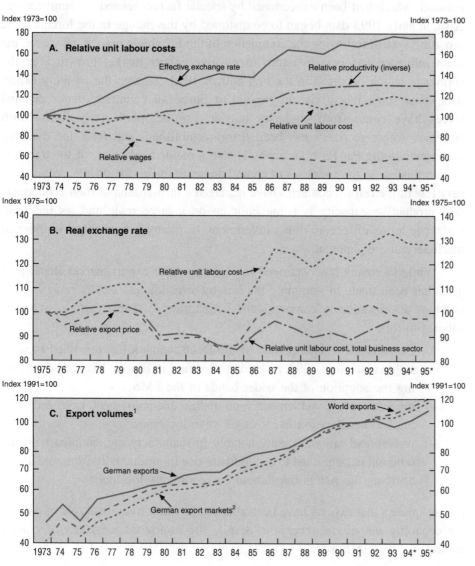

Diagram 3. **EXPORT COMPETITIVENESS IN MANUFACTURING IN WESTERN GERMANY**

Index 1973=100   Index 1973=100

A. Relative unit labour costs

Effective exchange rate   Relative productivity (inverse)

Relative unit labour cost

Relative wages

1973 74 75 76 77 78 79 80 81 82 83 84 85 86 87 88 89 90 91 92 93 94* 95*

Index 1975=100   Index 1975=100

B. Real exchange rate

Relative unit labour cost

Relative export price

Relative unit labour cost, total business sector

1975 76 77 78 79 80 81 82 83 84 85 86 87 88 89 90 91 92 93 94* 95*

Index 1991=100   Index 1991=100

C. Export volumes[1]

World exports

German exports

German export markets[2]

1973 74 75 76 77 78 79 80 81 82 83 84 85 86 87 88 89 90 91 92 93 94* 95*

* Projected data.
1. Total Germany; total goods.
2. A weighted average of import volumes in Germany's markets, with weights based on trade flows in 1991.
Source: OECD; IMF, *Balance of payments statistics;* Deutsche Bundesbank, *Monthly Report.*

17

To some extent, the rebound is a correction to the previous fall in export demand, which had been exacerbated by special factors related to reunification.[2] Also, in early 1993 data began to be distorted by the change in the foreign trade reporting system following the completion of the EC single market. However, the main influence has been a return to positive export market growth after the shrinkage which occurred in the first half of 1993. Though the monthly export data show some recent rise in exports to European countries, major demand forces have come from countries outside Europe, particularly from North America, where recovery has been firmly established, and from the dynamic economies in the Far East. Germany is also a major beneficiary of the transformation process in the countries of central and eastern Europe. While, so far, only very few of the reform countries have managed a turn-around of their economies, new productive capacity is being built up on a large scale and, as the main partner in terms of foreign direct investment, Germany is a principal supplier of machinery and equipment.

While Germany has continued to lose aggregate export market share, progress has been made in stemming the loss by arresting and slowly reversing the previous deterioration in competitiveness (Diagram 3). Three factors have contributed to this:

- the effective exchange rate of the Deutschemark has remained broadly stable since mid-1993, as currency turmoil in Europe has abated following the adoption of the wider bands in the EMS;
- moderate wage settlements and rising unemployment have led to a marked deceleration in effective wage increases;
- widespread rationalisation, notably in manufacturing, coupled with the rebound in output led to a significant rise in productivity from mid-1993, bringing the rise in unit labour costs virtually to a halt.

It thus appears that exports have been able to play their traditional role of pulling the economy out of the recession, despite the protracted weakness of crucial markets in western Europe.

Falling real household incomes cushioned by lower savings

For the first time in eleven years, private household consumption did not increase in 1993, but remained flat. It fell markedly early in the year, by 1¾ per cent (seasonally-adjusted), as a correction to the pre-emptive buying which occurred in late 1992 before the rise in the VAT rate, then rebounded, before falling again towards year-end. Faced with a substantial real increase in housing rent costs, households restrained spending on most other items, notably motor cars and foodstuffs. In restraining consumption, households were reacting to their more constrained income situation. Indeed, real disposable incomes fell for the first time in many years, as the effects of wage moderation and rising unemployment combined with persistent consumer price inflation. Nevertheless, households resisted the fall in real incomes, to some extent, by lowering savings (Diagram 4). The saving ratio, having declined by somewhat more than half a percentage point in 1992, fell by a further half point to 12$\frac{1}{4}$ per cent. From its peak in 1990 the saving ratio has now come down by about 1$\frac{1}{2}$ points, returning to the level of the years preceding unification and more than half way down to the level of the early 1980s.

The recent fall in the savings ratio corresponds to historical experience. As a rule, German consumers have tended to even out variations in income growth

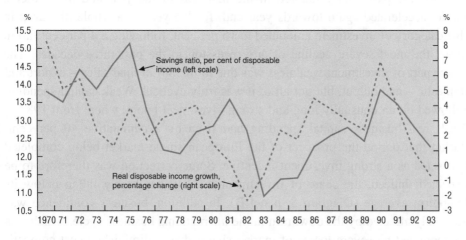

Diagram 4. **REAL DISPOSABLE INCOME AND HOUSEHOLD SAVING IN WESTERN GERMANY**[1]

1. Adjusted for extraordinary consumer expenditure in anticipation of the VAT increase on 1 January 1993.
Source: Deutsche Bundesbank and OECD.

19

over the business cycle.[3] But, they would only be expected to do so as long as they perceived an income decline as "cyclical", to be reversed soon, rather than "permanent" (due either to the risk of becoming unemployed or to a ratcheting-up of the tax burden). From this point of view, the unabated decline in the savings ratio is remarkable, given the severity of the recession and the related employment risks, as well as the certainty of an increasing tax burden. Certainly, lower interest rates and the re-introduction of the withholding tax on capital gains reduced the incentives to save. However, and perhaps more importantly, house-holds may have felt reassured by determined monetary and fiscal policy moves to safeguard price and currency stability and to bring public deficits and indebted-ness firmly under control. Thus, in contrast to the experience in the immediate aftermath of unification, a clear perspective that the remaining tasks of reunifica-tion would be coped with seems to have become visible in 1993. Moreover, greater confidence has appeared increasingly warranted by the broader-based nature of the upturn in eastern Germany.

Slump in business investment

1993 saw a sharp decline in west German business fixed investment of almost 7 per cent. It has been concentrated on machinery and equipment, where the fall was particularly marked in the first half of the year and then, after a pause, accelerated again towards year-end; for the year as a whole, the drop in this category of investment amounted to 15 per cent, following a 4 per cent fall in 1992, the most severe decline of any recession in the past three decades. The major part of investment weakness was due to the fall in final sales – export and domestic – and output, but not all of it was truly cyclical. Weak capital spending followed on an unusually long and strong investment boom, when, from 1987 to 1991, real business capital spending had risen by a cumulative 40 per cent; during that period the prospect of the European single market being completed had acted as a strong investment incentive. Some correction was therefore to be expected; indeed, the share of investment in GDP has barely fallen below its long-term average (Diagram 5, panel B). In addition, business confidence was adversely affected by the downturn in the international business cycle, which was compounded by severe losses of market shares due to diminished cost competi-tiveness. Remaining uncertainty about crucial elements in the policy environment also contributed towards undermining business confidence.

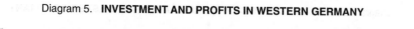

Diagram 5. **INVESTMENT AND PROFITS IN WESTERN GERMANY**

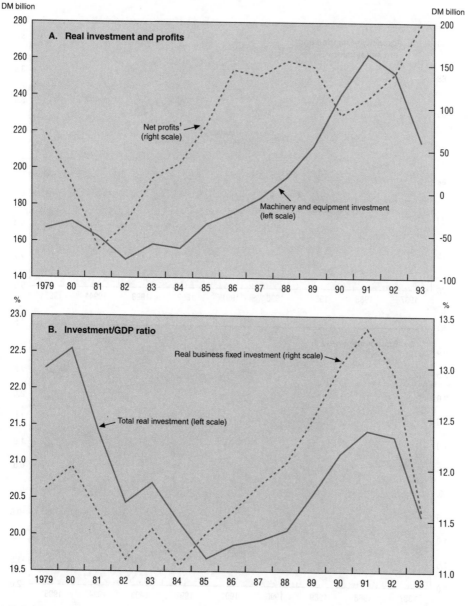

1. Defined as:

GDP — {(Compensation of employees) + (Interest costs) + (Depreciation) + (Indirect taxes - Subsidies)}.
Source: OECD estimates.

Diagram 6. **UTILISATION OF CAPITAL AND LABOUR IN WESTERN GERMANY**

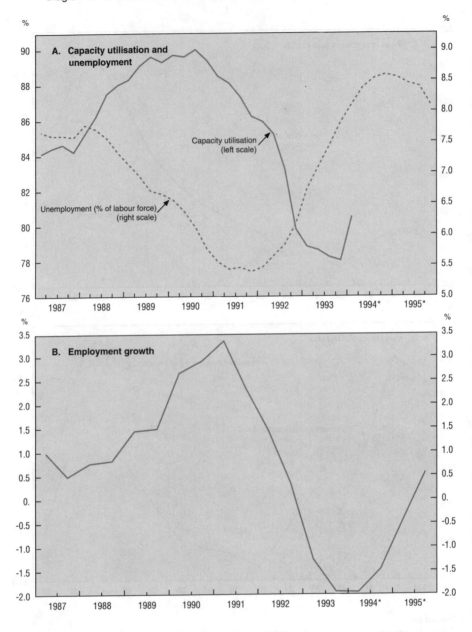

* Projected data.
Source: OECD and Ifo-Institut.

Nevertheless, in several respects the environment for business investment has become less gloomy in recent months. Moderate settlements in the spring wage round have dampened the rise in the wage bill and helped to bring the deterioration in competitiveness to a halt. At the same time, the squeeze in profits has induced firms to proceed with rationalisation in order to raise productivity. Hence, the rise in labour costs has virtually levelled-off for the whole economy and has probably been partly reversed in manufacturing. Moreover, as with personal consumption, firm policy commitments, particularly with respect to fiscal retrenchment and the need to abstain from further increasing of the tax burden as from 1995, have removed a major uncertainty from the investment climate (Diagram 6).

As is normal in a period of recession, profitability declined markedly in 1992 and 1993. For the manufacturing sector in particular, the profit situation apparently hit the record low of the early 1980s. However, profit margins in the overall economy have remained clearly higher than either in the 1975 or the 1982 recession.[4] Factors helping to mitigate the profit squeeze were a reduction in the costs of energy and other imports due to the higher exchange rate, the fall in long-term interest rates and, to some extent, the stabilisation of wage costs via lower settlements or personnel cuts. As noted in Part II, firms have been able to take advantage of lower long-term interest rates to restructure their finances, thus reducing, to some extent, the impact of short-term credit costs on their cash flow.

Eastern Germany: a broader based upturn

Progress in reconstruction

The reconstruction of the eastern German economy has made significant progress over the past two years. GDP in 1992 is estimated to have grown by almost 10 per cent. Following a temporary deceleration, activity re-gained strength in the second half of 1993, yielding an average rate of growth of about 7 per cent for the whole year. At the same time, there were encouraging signs that the upturn in the east is becoming more broadly based, if not yet self-sustained. Thus, 1993 saw a turnaround in manufacturing output, which rose markedly from the second quarter to year-end, when it grew by almost 9 per cent at annual rates. Between 1991 and 1993 eastern Germany's contribution to all-German GDP rose

23

from around 7 per cent to almost 10 per cent.[5] For the first time, production is rising faster than aggregate demand. Moreover, output, while previously concentrated on sectors benefiting from public investment, such as construction material and mechanical engineering has now extended to the production of motor vehicles, the chemical and electronics industries and textiles. Within the manufacturing sector, capital goods have shrunk from about a half of overall production to around two-fifths, with mechanical engineering, which in 1990 provided nearly a quarter of manufacturing output, falling to around 11 per cent by the end of 1992. Major growth sectors have been food and drinks, with significant investment in vehicle manufacturing and electrical engineering. And there have also been changes in enterprise structure, which is dominated by firms of 100 to 500 employees, but which also relies heavily on businesses with fewer than 20 employees.

Massive investment, totalling almost DM 140 billion, or roughly half of eastern German GDP, has begun to modernise the capital stock and improve the quality of supply: for the first time since unification, investment per capita in the east has exceeded that in the west. Private investment has continued to rise strongly, although the recession in the west had a dampening effect. Investment has thus become the most dynamic component of domestic demand, its share in GDP considerably exceeding the western German long-term trend. New firm registrations outnumbered closures and the Treuhandanstalt has nearly completed its task of privatisation. The number of enterprises still offered for sale by the Treuhandanstalt has been reduced to around 190 – 2 per cent of the original total – though some of these are relatively large.

Nevertheless, severe problems, both of demand and supply, still remain. As last year's *Survey* pointed out, the problem of aggregate demand is not so much its overall level as the split between foreign and domestic and between public and private demand, and the question of consumption versus investment. Table 3 shows that, despite the progress made, these basic problems remain. The share of exports in aggregate demand, including deliveries to the other part of Germany, is much lower than in the west – one-fifth compared with one-third. Of total domestic spending a major part is spent on imports, which are still almost as high as GDP, implying that east German output only covers slightly more than half of aggregate demand. Domestic demand, moreover, is heavily supported by the public sector, either via direct spending or via transfers to households.[6] Almost

Table 3. **Composition and financing of demand in eastern Germany**

DM billion

	1991	1992	1993
Total domestic demand	**358.5**	**431.3**	**487.9**
Public	108.4	124.8	137.2
Consumption	86.2	105.9	116.3
Investment	22.2	18.9	20.9
Private	250.2	306.5	350.8
Consumption	186.7	216.1	232.3
Investment	63.5	90.4	118.5
Financed by:	**358.5**	**431.3**	**487.9**
GDP	186.2	235.3	275.5
Public sector[1]	108.4	124.8	137.2
Private sector	77.8	110.5	138.3
Transfers to households	71.8	100.1	108.4
Capital inflow (residual)	100.5	95.9	104.0
Memorandum items:			
Capital account[2]	172.3	196.0	212.4
Current account[3]	−172.3	−196.0	−212.4
Exports	44.0	51.2	52.7
Imports	216.4	247.3	265.7

1. Assumes no leakage of public sector demand abroad and is thus only an approximation.
2. Defined as transfers to households plus capital inflow.
3. Defined as exports less imports of goods and services, national accounts basis.
Source: Statistisches Bundesamt, *Wirtschaft und Statististik.*

two-thirds of internal demand for domestic goods and services (*i.e.* total domestic demand minus imports) is generated by public consumption and investment spending. The remaining one-third is largely accounted for by that part of private domestic demand which cannot be satisfied abroad, *i.e.* purchases of services. Meanwhile, the household savings ratio has approached the western German level. While the share of private investment in total domestic demand of 24 per cent exceeds the corresponding figure in the west, it would need to be even higher in order to foster the catching-up process. Hence, too large a share of public transfers is currently being used for consumption.

Continued severe problems of competitiveness

The rise in household incomes has slowed markedly as the pace of wage convergence towards west German levels has moderated and unemployment has risen. On the other hand, the rate of price increase, while still considerably higher than in western Germany, decelerated to below 8 per cent, so that real disposable income remained broadly constant in 1993. In spite of the slowdown in wage convergence and the pick-up in productivity, the competitiveness problem remains essentially one of relative unit labour costs. Thus, whereas GDP per employee in the new Länder in 1993 was some 46 per cent of the level in the west, per capita wages and salaries rose to 70 per cent, implying eastern German unit wage costs some 44 per cent above those in western Germany – which themselves are among the highest in the world. Moreover, eastern Germany is being increasingly hard pressed by competition from neighbouring eastern countries, mainly Poland and the Czech Republic, where wages are much lower, even allowing for lower productivity. The prospects for profits, a crucial requirement for any self-sustained pick-up in private investment, are still gloomy in many sectors. Indeed, in 1993, total compensation of employees exceeded national income implying negative profits.[7] The major challenge is to achieve profitability by creating and expanding viable production rather than by further cuts in employment.

In this respect, other obstacles remain which by now are well known. Among the most important are marketing problems due not just to poor product quality and specification but also to the absence of distribution networks or lack of marketing know-how. A further impediment arises from deficiencies in human capital, especially managerial skills. Remaining deficiencies in the physical infrastructure pose a further competitive problem, as do the costs of actual and prospective administrative delays, still unsettled property claims and the environmental clean-up burden. On all these aspects, progress in removing these obstacles is difficult to assess, but without a substantial improvement in infrastructure the observed industrial take-off would not have been possible.

The main problem remaining is the persistent lack of an export base. Eastern German exports (including sales to western Germany) have stabilised, but at a low level. Part of those goods which have been delivered to the western Länder were "supported" by various measures, such as the preference given to eastern supplies in public procurement. The major reason for this is lack of competitiveness. In particular, high wage costs not only discourage private investment and make privatisation of the remaining firms difficult, they also drive up unemployment to unnecessarily high levels. The need for continued large unemployment payments perpetuates public transfers from the west to the east, inhibits a shift of such transfers from consumption to investment purposes and adds to the danger of the eastern Länder remaining underdeveloped (the *"mezzogiorno* problem"). Higher competitiveness of eastern manufacturing is therefore the key to success for both the convergence process and all-German fiscal consolidation.

The labour market and inflation

Employment deterioration in the west – stabilisation in the east

Western German employment headed downwards in mid-1992, declined by more than 1³/₄ per cent in 1993, on a year-average basis, and continued falling into early 1994. Since the previous cyclical peak two years ago, the number of workers and employees has fallen by more than ³/₄ million, corresponding to 2¹/₂ per cent of the labour force. The decline has been concentrated in manufacturing (–5¹/₂ per cent), particularly the investment goods sector, which was hit hardest both by the recession abroad and by the loss in competitiveness, which forced it to labour-saving rationalisation. Slackening consumer demand also caused a decline in employment in trade and transportation, whereas construction employment kept rising, albeit slightly. Although employment in most service industries, particularly financial, legal and personal services, continued expanding (by 1¹/₂ per cent annual average), this could not offset the labour shakeout in the other sectors.

Labour supply receded slightly in 1993, as the inflow of foreign workers levelled off and discouraged job-seekers dropped out of the labour force. Nevertheless, registered unemployment rose by almost ¹/₂ million to average 2.3 million or 7.4 per cent of the labour force. The number of workers on short-time almost quadrupled in the early stage of the recession, hitting a high of over 1 million in early 1993 (not seasonally adjusted), but fell back to half that level as the business outlook in the export-oriented sector improved. An encouraging sign has been the marked rise in job vacancies in early 1994, but unemployment is continuing to rise, as scope for productivity gains exists in many sectors; labour productivity in the total economy declined by ¼ per cent in 1993. Even in manufacturing, productivity growth stalled.

Following the massive shedding of labour and the rebound in output, employment in eastern Germany stopped falling towards mid-1993, remaining constant thereafter, at a level still 3 per cent below a year earlier. The year-on-year decline mainly concerned short-time workers, while full-time employment remained stable. The sharp reduction in protected jobs (public works, retraining etc.) during the year was thus not reflected in overall employment. The labour shakeout in manufacturing has been more or less completed; new hiring remains very strong (at double-digit annual rates) in construction, but is losing momentum in private services where the first "wave" of pent-up demand seems to have been by and large satisfied. Registered unemployment seems to have levelled-off at a rate slightly above 15 per cent, corresponding to almost 1.2 million people (Table 4). However, short-time work, training measures, public works ("*Arbeitsbeschaffungsmaßnahmen*") and early retirement prevented a further 1.6 million persons from being unemployed in 1993, although this figure was some 15 per cent lower than a year earlier. Apart from early retirement, labour

Table 4. **Labour market trends in eastern and western Germany**

In '000 persons

	Western Germany			Eastern Germany		
	1991	1992	1993	1991	1992	1993
Labour force	30 682	30 949	30 922	8 422	7 879	7 632
Unemployed	1 689	1 808	2 270	913	1 170	1 149
Resident employees	28 993	29 141	28 652	7 509	6 709	6 483
of which:						
Self-employed	3 044	3 055	3 046	362	411	445
Dependent	25 949	26 086	25 606	7 147	6 298	6 038
Commuters	234	346	362	−290	−365	−355
Employment	29 227	29 487	29 014	7 219	6 344	6 128
of which:						
Public works	..	..	..	183	388	260
Short-time work	..	..	..	1 616	370	182
Memorandum item:						
Unemployment rate (%)	5.5	5.8	7.3	10.8	14.8	15.1

Source: Statistisches Bundesamt; Federal Labour Office; calculations by the six economic research institutes.

force participation has dropped substantially. Thus, the female participation ratio, previously one of the highest in the world, has come down to the relatively low western German level.

Disinflation gathering momentum

Given the severity of the recession, domestic wage moderation, stable or even falling world commodity prices and the appreciation of the Deutschemark, progress towards price stability was disappointingly slow in 1993. On average the western German inflation rate, as measured by the consumer price index, actually edged up to 4.2 per cent in 1993. However, from mid-year, disinflation gained momentum, with the year-over-year rise in the CPI falling by a whole percentage point between July 1993 and April 1994, to a rate of 3.1 per cent.

At the same time, the gap between production cost developments and consumer price inflation has widened (Diagram 7). Thus, the rise in manufacturing unit labour costs has abated, labour shedding causing productivity to rebound and contributing towards markedly lower wage increases than in the past two years.

Diagram 7. **PRODUCER VERSUS CONSUMER PRICE TRENDS**

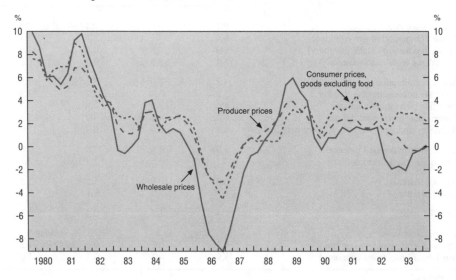

Source: OECD, *Main Economic Indicators.*

29

Continued low energy and raw materials prices, combined with an effective appreciation in the Deutschemark, led to a second year of falling import prices. Together with sluggish demand and stronger competitive pressure on foreign and domestic markets this helped contain producer prices, which actually fell marginally in 1993.

Unlike manufacturing, in the services sector, where consumer demand has proved more resistant and where competition is traditionally less pronounced, the cost push from the past wage round was passed through to prices. Thus, service prices rose by over 6 per cent, even faster than in 1992. A similar acceleration took place in rents, reflecting the housing shortage.[8] In addition, and partly reflected in higher service and housing costs, states and local communities raised a broad range of administered prices and public charges. Such increases were the consequence both of price increases being held back in previous years and of more market-related pricing behaviour on the part of public authorities, in part

Table 5. **Inflation in a snapshot**

Percentage changes at annual rates

	1992	1993	1994[1]	1995[1]
Private wage rate	9.4	3.6	2.1	2.6
Private compensation per employee	9.4	4.2	3.4	3.1
Labour productivity (total economy)	3.9	0.8	4.1	2.3
Unit labour costs (total economy)	5.4	3.5	−0.7	0.2
Private consumption deflator	4.7	4.0	3.1	1.9
Government consumption deflator	5.9	3.4	1.7	1.8
Total fixed investment deflator	4.4	2.9	2.8	2.7
Construction investment deflator	6.3	4.2	3.9	3.8
Machinery and equipment investment deflator	1.9	0.6	0.9	1.0
Final domestic demand deflator	4.9	3.6	2.8	2.0
Total domestic demand deflator	4.7	3.6	2.8	2.1
Export deflator	0.7	0.8	1.5	1.5
Import deflator	−1.7	−1.0	1.1	1.7
Terms of trade	2.4	1.7	0.4	−0.2
Memorandum items:				
Real total compensation per employee	4.5	0.2	0.2	1.2
Real labour costs (total economy)	3.9	0.2	0.5	1.0

1. Projected.
Source: OECD.

because of the need to reduce public deficits. Finally, the increase in the standard VAT rate to 15 per cent as from January 1993 added ½ percentage point to the year-over-year inflation rate, while the higher mineral oil tax had a similar effect at the beginning of 1994. Abstracting from these tax-induced price adjustments, the underlying rate of inflation has come down to around 2½ per cent (Table 5).

In eastern Germany, price increases remained strong until 1993, the annual rate of almost 8 per cent being twice as high as in the western part of the country. Most of the rise came at the beginning of the year when landlords were authorised to increase rents and many other directly or indirectly administered prices were also raised, bringing them closer to western German levels. The pace of inflation during the year was only a little faster than in the west and in early 1994 the rate was barely ¼ percentage point higher.

Stabilisation of the current account

Rising trade surplus offset by deficit on invisibles

Following the large swings in the foreign trade and services balances in the years immediately after reunification, the current account has remained broadly stable, exhibiting a deficit in 1992 and 1993 of around DM 35 billion, equivalent to 1 per cent of GDP. The trade surplus widened considerably in 1993 (from DM 49 to 75 billion), mainly towards year-end, when exports picked up while domestic demand relapsed. However, at the same time, the deficit on invisibles soared to over DM 100 billion (Table 6). Three factors were behind this: a further rise in net tourism imports, where pent-up demand by eastern Germans added to the secular upward trend in west German tourism demand, reinforcing the effects of the real appreciation of the Deutschemark and a marked reduction in air fares; a continued fall in net investment income, reflecting both the decline in (net) foreign assets as a consequence of the swing to current account deficit, and changes in interest rate differentials; and lower military receipts, with the withdrawal of foreign troops.

Capital inflows hitting record high

Long-term capital transactions in 1993 yielded a net inflow of around DM 190 billion, which not only far exceeded the current account deficit, but, by

Table 6. **The current account of the balance of payments**

DM billion

	1990	1991	1992	1993
Trade balance	**+118.6**	**+38.1**	**+49.3**	**+72.5**
Exports	662.0	665.8	671.2	604.0
Imports	543.5	627.7	621.9	531.5[1]
Adjustment	−1.6	+1.4	+0.7	−4.1
Services	−4.8	−13.3	−34.4	−52.0[1]
of which:				
Investment income	+28.2	+32.1	+24.5	+15.0
Tourism	−30.7	−34.2	−39.9	−44.6
Transfers	−36.5	−58.5	−50.0	−51.7
of which:				
Net contribution to the EU	−11.6	−19.1	−22.0	−23.6
Other public transfers	−13.3	−27.7	−14.5	−14.6
Current account	**+75.7**	**−32.2**	**−34.4**	**−35.2**

1. Partly estimated.
Source: Deutsche Bundesbank.

more than quadrupling from 1992, attained unprecedented levels. Throughout the year, the interest of foreign investors was stimulated by the positive interest-rate differential on German long-term bonds *vis-à-vis* the United States, coupled with expectations of lower rates, and reinforced at times by currency speculation. Around two-thirds of new bond issues notionally went to foreign portfolios. However, to a considerable extent, inflows were accounted for by a "recycling" of domestic savings placed abroad in order to avoid the withholding tax introduced at the beginning of the year (see next chapter). While there was for the first time since 1989 rising foreign interest in the German stock market, thereby supporting the buoyancy of share prices, inward foreign direct investment stagnated. At the same time that capital imports surged, German capital exports declined (to around DM 97 billion). This was largely due to the reduced attraction of foreign investment certificates, as capital gains on these instruments were made tax liable.

Short-term capital exports of private non-banks rose substantially in 1993 (by around DM 60 billion), mainly in the form of private investments with foreign banks. As the net outflow was concentrated on the beginning of the year

Table 7. **The capital account of the balance of payments**

DM billion

	1990	1991	1992	1993
Long-term capital	**−65.4**	**−27.3**	**+39.7**	**+186.5**
Exports	−106.6	−95.9	−116.8	−97.0
Direct investment	−37.4	−38.0	−27.7	−19.3
Securities	−22.9	−27.3	−70.4	−40.3
Bank loans	−43.0	−26.2	−14.2	−32.4
Other	−3.3	−4.4	−4.5	−4.9
Imports	+41.2	+68.6	+156.5	+283.4
Direct investment	+4.1	+7.1	+3.8	−0.5
Securities	+15.3	+61.7	+123.8	+241.7
Bank loans	+22.1	+0.0	+29.3	+42.7
Other	−0.3	−0.2	−0.3	−0.4
Short-term capital of non-banks	**+0.3**	**+20.2**	**−0.4**	**−84.4**
Enterprises and households	−19.3	+11.1	+3.6	−60.5
Public authorities	−5.0	−3.8	−7.3	−2.6
Other payment items [1]	+24.6	+12.9	+3.3	−21.3
Short-term capital of banks	**+0.4**	**+39.7**	**+63.8**	**−102.6**
Valuation adjustment of Bundesbank foreign asset position	−5.1	+0.5	−6.3	+1.5
Change in Bundesbank net foreign assets	**+5.9**	**+0.8**	**+62.4**	**−34.2**

1. Net errors and omissions.
Source: Deutsche Bundesbank.

and abated thereafter, it was probably also motivated primarily by tax avoidance. However, these outflows were by far exceeded by the net long-term inflow, allowing the net short-term foreign assets of German banks to rise by around DM 100 billion (Table 7).

Short-term projections

The OECD projections for 1994 and 1995 embody the following main assumptions (Table 8). Foreign markets, particularly in continental Europe, are likely to strengthen as they come out of recession, while cost-competitiveness in

Table 8. **Projections**

Percentage changes unless otherwise noted; volumes in 1991 prices

	1993	1994	1995
A. International and policy assumptions			
World market growth	0.7	5.5	6.8
Relative unit labour costs in manufacturing[1]	4.7	−3.6	−0.5
Change in cyclically-adjusted deficit[2]	1.4	0.8	0.1
Short-term interest rates	7.3	5.1	4.3
Long-term interest rates	6.5	6.4	6.1

	Total Germany			West Germany			East Germany		
	1993	1994	1995	1993	1994	1995	1993	1994	1995
B. Demand and output									
Private consumption	0.1	−0.2	0.9	−0.0	−0.4	0.9	1.5	0.9	1.0
Government consumption	−0.7	−0.1	0.1	−1.3	0.0	0.4	2.6	−0.6	−1.3
Gross fixed investment	−3.3	4.1	6.0	−6.9	1.4	3.0	15.6	15.4	17.3
Construction	3.1	4.9	4.9	−0.5	2.3	2.0	21.2	15.9	15.6
Machinery and equipment	−11.4	2.8	7.7	−15.0	0.1	4.5	8.1	14.7	19.8
Change in stocks[3]	−0.6	0.2	0.2	−0.7	0.1	0.1	0.6	1.8	0.9
Total domestic demand	−1.4	1.0	2.2	−2.6	0.2	1.4	6.0	5.9	6.3
Exports of goods and services	−9.5	4.4	7.4	−6.1	4.4	7.0	−1.0	15.2	16.5
Imports of goods and services	−10.0	1.1	5.8	−9.5	1.8	6.5	3.6	5.1	6.5
Change in foreign balance[3]	0.2	0.7	0.4	0.6	1.0	0.7	−4.8	−2.4	−3.2
GDP at constant prices	−1.3	1.8	2.6	−1.9	1.2	2.0	7.1	9.1	8.8
C. Other macroeconomic variables									
Unemployment rate[4]	8.9	10.0	10.0	7.3	8.4	8.4	15.8	16.8	16.9
GDP deflator	3.9	2.8	2.0	3.3	2.5	1.7	10.3	4.8	4.0
Private consumption deflator	4.0	3.1	1.9	3.4	2.8	1.5	7.9	5.1	4.0
Household saving ratio[5]	12.1	11.3	11.1	12.3	11.5	11.1	11.4	10.5	11.0
Current balance[2]	−1.1	−0.7	−0.2						

1. In a common currency; total Germany proxied by western Germany.
2. As a percentage of nominal GDP.
3. As a percentage of real GDP in the previous period.
4. As a percentage of the labour force.
5. As a percentage of disposable income.
Source: OECD.

Germany is set to improve slightly as overall wage trends bring the rise in unit labour costs to a temporary halt. On the policy front, the underlying assumptions are that:

- A restrictive fiscal stance will be maintained throughout the projection period, with the cyclically-adjusted general government deficit being cut by 1.8 per cent of GDP.
- Short-term interest rates should continue declining throughout 1994, bottoming out in early 1995 at around 4¼ per cent. Long-term rates, having moved up to over 7 per cent in line with the international firming on bond yields are unlikely to come down substantially, so that the yield curve is set to steepen which, indeed, would be normal during a period of recovery.

With export growth accelerating, and remaining the driving force of the recovery, overall real GDP is expected to expand by 1¾ per cent in 1994, rising to 2½ per cent in 1995, western German growth being projected to reach 1¼ and 2 per cent respectively.

With output rising, capacity utilisation in manufacturing will increase. Profits should thus recover, in part because of recent rationalisation efforts. These factors should in turn, work to reverse the decline in business fixed investment. Capital spending is expected to remain particularly buoyant in eastern Germany and to concentrate more on industrial machinery and equipment, following the strong pick-up in output growth during 1993. As wage growth decelerates and productivity converges towards western German levels, the stage could be set for an improvement in competitiveness in the eastern Länder.

The recovery in output will be reflected in the labour market only with a lag, as firms initially absorb accumulated spare capacity. Thus, employment may continue declining throughout 1994 and pick up only towards mid-1995. By that time, registered unemployment may have peaked at a rate of 10 per cent of the labour force (over 8 per cent in western Germany). With labour slack remaining significant, wage growth is likely to remain modest in 1995, allowing consumer price inflation to abate from a current annual rate of 3 per cent to about 1¾ per cent towards the end of the forecasting period.

Private consumption may be a lagging component in the recovery of domestic demand. Under the impact of declining employment, wage moderation and cuts in social benefits, real disposable income is expected to fall by 1 per cent in 1994. The re-introduction of the 7.5 per cent ''solidarity'' income tax surcharge at the beginning of 1995 will constitute a further drag. Nevertheless, the decline in households' purchasing power will bottom out as inflation subsides. This should eventually boost consumer confidence and induce households to increase spending.

Since the recovery is expected to be export-led and domestic demand to remain flat for most of 1994, the real foreign balance should make a substantial contribution to the resumption of GDP growth. Allowing for the improvement in the terms of trade which has stemmed from the effective appreciation of the Deutschemark, the current account deficit may shrink markedly, to less than DM 10 billion or about ¼ per cent of GDP in 1995.

While present projections are still for a gradual and somewhat uneven recovery, the balance of risks appears to have shifted somewhat. A downward risk still attaches to domestic demand, where falling real incomes and rising unemployment may induce consumers to higher (precautionary) saving. But recent leading indicators suggest both the possibility of greater export buoyancy and an unexpected resilience on the part of consumers. In this event, a stronger than expected pick-up in profits could encourage higher private investment. Another risk relates to strong liquidity growth in recent years. Actual inflation may be easing partly because liquidity is fuelling the demand for financial assets rather than for goods and services. Therefore a too rapid economic recovery could militate against a further decline in consumer price inflation.

II.   Monetary policy

Overview

Monetary conditions have been cautiously eased as wage and price inflation pressures have abated. But the pace of interest rate reduction has been rather slow, since monetary overshooting and the consequent liquidity overhang have been giving more ambivalent signals about possible future inflation. In these circumstances, the Bundesbank has sought to avoid any possible adverse effects on the exchange rate or bond market confidence by exerting a steadying influence on interest rate movements for extended periods. Moreover, from a domestic point of view, pressure for more aggressive monetary easing has been less acute than from an international one, because long-term rates, which are more important for investment decisions in Germany, had fallen to a little above their all-time low of 5.8 per cent by January 1994.[9] They have risen more recently, in line with the international trend, and the pace of central bank interest-rate reduction has subsequently continued steepening the yield curve. On balance, however, the presumption built into the OECD projections is that further disinflation will leave room for additional short-term interest rate reductions.

This chapter begins with an overview of the inflation background to monetary policy-making, including the role of Deutschemark stability and wage and public sector cost developments. It then discusses the monetary easing process in the light of the overshooting of monetary targets, and analyses the stance of monetary policy in the light of recent monetary and bond market developments.

Disinflation and the Deutschemark

In contrast to previous recessions, the inflationary imbalances responsible for the 1992-93 downturn were domestically-generated: excess demand associ-

37

ated with unification generated wage pressures; and public sector expansion drove up public service charges and indirect taxes (Diagram 8). Labour-market and budgetary developments have thus been the key factors in the subsequent disinflation and monetary relaxation processes. External factors have nevertheless played a role. Weaker raw material and energy prices, combined with a general firmness in the effective rate of the Deutschemark, have actually resulted in a falling import price deflator. And the Bundesbank has consistently adhered to the concept of Deutschemark stability as a *sine qua non* of financial market confidence in monetary policy, particularly in view of the overshooting of monetary targets.

Firmness of the Deutschemark

As noted above, a significant easing in inflationary pressures is evident from the virtual elimination of inflation at the producer and the wholesale levels, due to weak commodity prices, which fell by 3 per cent, on average, in 1993, and an effective appreciation of the Deutschemark. According to the OECD trade-weighted index, the effective rate of the Deutschemark was 7 per cent higher in 1993 than the average for 1991 and this tended to moderate domestic price rises (Diagram 9, panel A). Most of the appreciation actually occurred in 1992. During 1993 the German currency tended to appreciate against the European currencies, particularly immediately after the enlargement of the fluctuation margins in the EMS in early August. However, once speculative pressures had abated, most currencies moved in the opposite direction during the autumn and winter, the net result being that the Deutschemark was quoted only $1^{1}/_{2}$ per cent higher on average against the ERM currencies in the first quarter of 1994 than it had been during the same period of 1993. Moreover, between late autumn and early February 1994, the Deutschemark was under downward pressure against the dollar, and this was of concern to the Bundesbank, influencing the timing of interest rate cuts. More recently, though, in spite of the tightening of United States monetary policy in the first half of 1994, and the associated narrowing in Deutschemark-dollar interest rate differentials, the dollar has weakened against the DM (panel B) and this has relieved possible pressure on monetary policy from this source.

Diagram 8. **INFLATION INDICATORS**

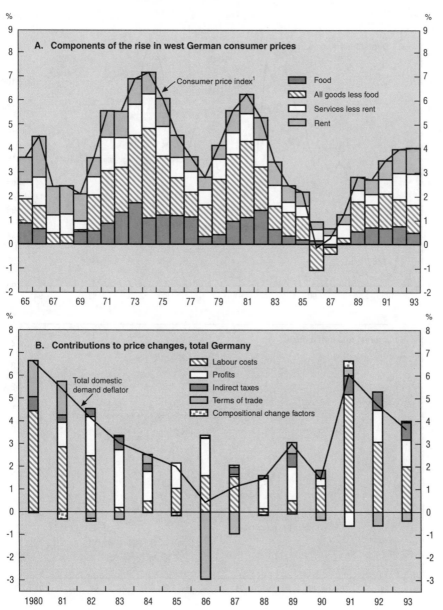

1. Annual percentage change.
Source: OECD, *Main Economic Indicators* and *National Accounts*.

Diagram 9. **EXCHANGE RATE DEVELOPMENTS AND INTEREST RATE DIFFERENTIALS**

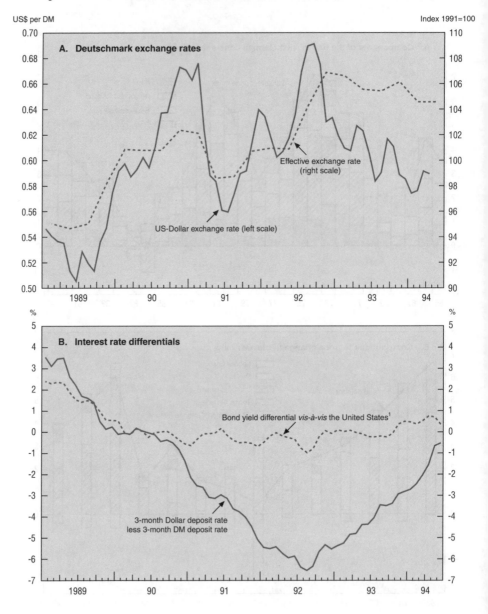

1. Composite of over 10 year government bonds for the United States, 7-15 year public sector bonds for Germany.
Source: OECD.

Domestic sources of disinflation

At the consumer level, services and rents have been the major factors sustaining inflation, the twelve-month rate of inflation falling only from 4.3 per cent in July 1993 to 3.7 per cent in December. Furthermore, taxes, charges, contributions and other administered prices were raised in 1993, reflecting the need to pay for previous public pay increases. Decelerating wage growth, reinforced by a significant rebound in labour productivity, will be the main factor driving inflation down, the 1993 wage round being considerably lower than the previous two, and the 1994 pay agreements opening up the prospect of a return to price stability.[10] In this respect, the wage settlement in the chemical industry, which applies to 700 000 employees, marked a major breakthrough for the 1994 wage round. The agreement, valid for fifteen months (November 1993 to January 1995) allows for a three-month wage freeze, followed by a 2 per cent increase. Overall, recent private sector wage settlements suggest that average contractual wage increases will slow to about 2 per cent in 1994, down from an estimated 3½ per cent in 1993.

The very moderate pay round for civil servants will also have a beneficial effect on inflation in the public sector, where the public consumption deflator is expected to rise by under 2 per cent, compared with 6 per cent in 1992. Administrative price and tax increases will also tend to diminish in effect. Abstracting from the impact of large administrative price increases and the mineral oil tax hike of 1 January 1994, the annual rate of inflation would have been around 2½ per cent in the beginning of 1994. As these effects on the price level pass through, the inflation rate should thus subside by about ½ percentage point from this source alone. Service prices and rents, the two most stubborn components of inflation, will continue to rise faster than the average inflation rate in 1993, due to structural factors such as a low exposure of services to foreign competition and excess demand in the housing market. However, both continue to edge down. On a twelve-month basis, service price rises slowed down from 7½ per cent in June to 6 per cent in December, and rents fell from 6 per cent to 5 per cent.

The monetary easing process

Stubbornly high M3 growth

Since 1988, the key intermediate target has been M3, the target growth of which has been derived from the Bundesbank's long-term inflation objective of

0 to 2 per cent, plus potential output growth and a velocity trend (Table 9). In practice, the Bundesbank has normally used a target range of 2 or 3 percentage points, rather than a single number, in order to allow for temporary factors – such as indirect tax increases – which can affect the short-run relationship between money and prices.

In setting the 1993 monetary target, the Bundesbank retained its 2 per cent long-run inflation benchmark, while assuming a 3 per cent increase in output potential. Together with an allowance for the downward trend in velocity, this implied a monetary expansion of 6 per cent on average. However, taking into account the perceived liquidity overhang in the economy at the end of 1992, the growth in the money stock was fixed at $4^{1}/_{2}$ to $6^{1}/_{2}$ per cent between the fourth quarter of 1992 and the fourth quarter of 1993 (Diagram 10).

Despite the modest increase in nominal GDP, M3 grew at an average rate of 7.4 per cent between the fourth quarters of 1992 and 1993, exceeding the top end of the target range by a significant margin. This overshooting was partly due to special factors, such as changes in tax laws. More fundamentally, however, monetary growth reflected strong credit expansion, sustained by both public and private demand, with public sector credit (including the railways, Post Office and Treuhand agency) being largely based on securitised borrowing from the banks

Table 9. **Monetary targets and money growth**

Percentage change

	1992	1993	1994
Setting of monetary targets			
Potential output (a)	$2^{3}/_{4}$	3	$2^{1}/_{2}$
Normative inflation (b)	2	2	2
Trend income velocity (c)	$-^{1}/_{2}$	-1	-1
M3 (a) + (b) – (c)	$5^{1}/_{4}$	6	$5^{1}/_{2}$
Target range [1]	$3^{1}/_{2}$-$5^{1}/_{2}$	$4^{1}/_{2}$-$6^{1}/_{2}$	4-6
Outcome			
M3 [1]	9.4	7.4	
Nominal GDP	7.5	2.6	
Income velocity (GDP/M3)	-1.9	-4.8	

1.   Fourth quarter of the current year compared to fourth quarter of the previous year.
Source: Deutsche Bundesbank.

Diagram 10. **MONEY SUPPLY DEVELOPMENTS**

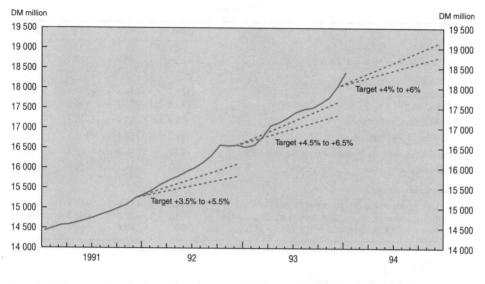

DM million

19 500
19 000
18 500
18 000
17 500
17 000
16 500
16 000
15 500
15 000
14 500
14 000

Target +4% to +6%

Target +4.5% to +6.5%

Target +3.5% to +5.5%

1991   92   93   94

Source: OECD.

and that of the private sector concentrated on long-term fixed rate loans, which were highly attractive for borrowers (Table 10). At the same time, monetary capital formation (embracing *inter alia* longer-term deposits not included in M3) was weak, so that monetary expansion was primarily a reflection of domestic factors in 1993.[11]

The monetary target for 1994, at 4 to 6 per cent, has been set slightly lower than that for 1993, reflecting a lower estimation of potential output growth. However, the money supply continued to overshoot the target range by a wide margin at the beginning of 1994. A significant source of distortion was the overhang arising from the sharp increase in monetary growth at the end of 1993, mainly due to changes in tax legislation. Interest income from German holdings in foreign-based investment funds was made subject to German withholding tax with effect from 1 January and this triggered an anticipatory repatriation of offshore funds held in Luxembourg as these instruments lost appeal.[12] In addition, however, credit demand continued to be strong, while uncertainties about

43

Table 10. **The expansion of the money supply and its counterparts**

DM billion

	1990	1991	1992	1993
Money stock (M3) (1 + 2 – 3 – 4 – 5)	+66.9	+95.6	+117.1	+186.2
1. Credits to:				
Private sector	+181.7	+259.3	+247.9	+243.7
Public sector	+41.6	+26.7	+46.3	+96.3
2. Net foreign asset formation	+48.4	–7.4	–40.7	–5.5
3. Monetary capital formation [1]	+161.3	+154.4	+101.5	+98.2
4. Central bank deposits of domestic public authorities	+12.3	–6.4	–12.3	+13.1
5. Other items, net	+31.1	+35.1	+52.9	+31.2
M3 and its components				
Currency in circulation and sight deposits (M1)	+44.5	+17.6	+63.3	+55.2
Time deposits maturing in less than four years (M2 – M1)	+73.1	+77.2	+46.5	+66.0
Saving deposits with three-months notice (M3 – M2)	+50.7	+0.8	+7.4	+65.0

1. Time deposits for four years and over; savings deposits at over three-months notice; bank savings bonds; bank bonds outstanding.
Source: Deutsche Bundesbank, *Monthly Report.*

long-term interest rates, which arose from February onwards, continued to depress demand for longer-term financial assets.

Gradual interest rate reduction

While monetary indicators receive special attention given the possible longer-run consequences for inflation, any short-run failure to meet the monetary target does not lead to an automatic response from the Bundesbank. This pragmatic approach is reflected in the fact that interest rates have been lowered despite substantial monetary overshooting, suggesting that inflation prospects have been given equal or superior weight to the M3 aggregate. Relaxation was initially prompted by the *de facto* appreciation of the Deutschemark in the September 1992 ERM realignment. The sluggish growth of M3 at the beginning of 1993, owing to the reversal of special factors[13] made it easier for the Bundesbank to continue the policy of cautiously easing interest rates, with the discount rate being cut from 8.25 per cent in January to 6.75 per cent in July. While the decline in the discount rate was interrupted during the summer, the repurchase rate fell close to the discount rate during the ERM crisis. Subsequently, the appreciation of the DM within the ERM following the August adjustment, together with the agreement on a fiscal consolidation programme and a moderation in the pace of monetary growth, allowed the Bundesbank to resume monetary easing of the discount rate, which was cut by 1 percentage point, in total, in September and October.

From the end of October 1993 until mid-February, when it cut the discount rate by $\frac{1}{2}$ a percentage point, the Bundesbank paused in its strategy of gradual interest rate reductions (Diagram 11, panel A). This was against market expectations and was due not just to the reacceleration in monetary growth but also to the unsettled fiscal and labour-market environment. To contain such "at times rather euphoric" expectations of interest rate cuts in the money market, the Bundesbank made greater use, within the framework of its securities repurchase transactions, of the instrument of the fixed-rate tender.

The cautious stance can also be partially traced to the perceived need to avoid causing agitation in the foreign exchange market. The internationalisation of the Deutschemark has made exchange rate developments increasingly dependent on foreign investor confidence. Although the Deutschemark has been relatively strong within the ERM, the periodic downward pressure against the dollar during the autumn of 1993 was seen as heightening the risk that monetary accommodation could lead to a large shift out of DM assets by foreign investors. More generally, the authorities have taken the view that more aggressive action to reduce interest rates could jeopardise the credibility of the commitment to price stability and entail adverse effects on long-term interest rates. By the beginning of January 1994, bond yields had fallen to 5.8 per cent (for 7 to 15-year bonds), which was viewed as a mark of confidence in the stance of monetary policy.[14] In these circumstances the Bundesbank considered that there was "little to be gained in terms of business cycle policy if the reduction in short-term rates were accompanied by a significant increase in long-term rates".

The improving budget outlook, a firming of the DM at the beginning of 1994 and the satisfactory wage-settlement outcome prompted the Bundesbank to resume its policy of gradual easing from February 1994 onwards. While the discount rate has been cut from 5.75 to 4.5 per cent, the repurchase rate has declined from 6 per cent in February to 5 per cent in June. By contrast, German long-term interest rates have subsequently risen, largely reflecting international linkage between bond markets (see below).

Diagram 11. **INTEREST RATE DEVELOPMENTS**

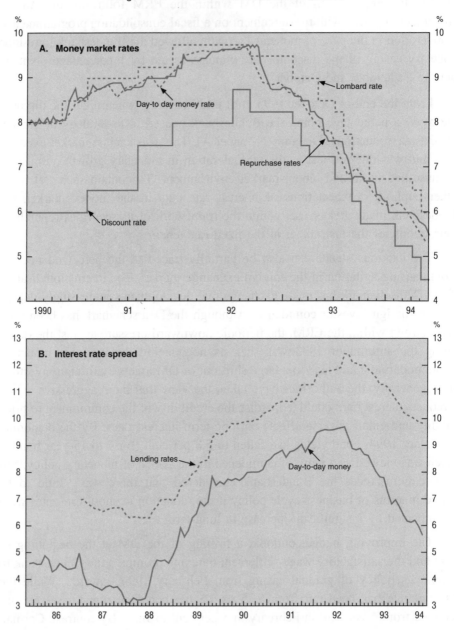

Source: OECD and Deutsche Bundesbank, *Monthly Report.*

The interpretation of monetary stance

Significance of M3 developments

The Bundesbank views monetary policy as having a major impact on inflation with a lag of two to three years. The conceptual framework for its policy formulation is in broad accordance with a modern form of the quantity theory of money in which monetary growth in excess of potential output growth is perceived as raising the "equilibrium" price level – the so-called P* (*P-star*).[15] According to statistical evidence the actual price level adjusts to the new equilibrium with a lag of about ten quarters (Diagram 12). This would normally imply adjusting the stance of policy in anticipation of potential inflation pressure as well as recorded price movements.

However, the reliability of M3 as an intermediate monetary indicator has been reduced by a large variety of "special factors", such as portfolio adjustments in east Germany after the introduction of the Deutschemark, changes in the legislation on interest income taxation, and speculative currency flows during the periods of ERM turmoil. While the Bundesbank can, in principle, use money-market operations to sterilise the impact of exchange market interventions on bank liquidity, it is virtually impossible to prevent money from abroad flowing to domestic non banks and hence boosting the money supply. Recently, residents have repatriated to Germany a significant part of their savings in Luxembourg-based investment funds. However, increased uncertainties about the future movement of interest rates in the capital market prompted investors to lodge funds in time deposit accounts.

The value of an intermediate target rests also on the ability of the monetary authorities to control it, at least indirectly. In principle, higher interest rates can affect money demand via two channels: by raising the opportunity cost of holding money – for a given level of income – and by "crowding out" aggregate demand. However, overshooting of the target range over the last three years may be partly explained by the fact that high interest rates, associated with an inverted yield curve, have induced portfolio shifts into more liquid assets, thus boosting rather than dampening broad money growth. Two factors in particular have induced portfolio adjustments out of long-term assets (including monetary capital) and into relatively liquid assets contained in M3:

Diagram 12. **LONG-RUN MONEY/INFLATION RELATIONSHIP
IN WESTERN GERMANY**

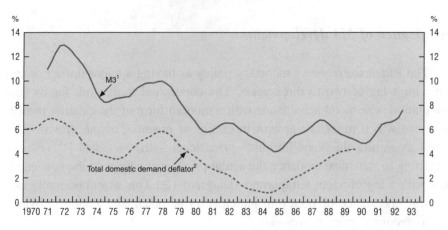

1. Annual rate of growth smoothed with 10-quarter moving average.
2. Annual rate of growth smoothed with 10-quarter moving average and lagged 10 quarters.
Source: Deutsche Bundesbank and OECD.

– Anticipation of the introduction on 1 January 1993 of a 30 per cent
withholding tax on interest income earned by domestic residents induced
a sharp rise in currency in circulation around the end of 1992. (However,
the implications of the boost in currency in circulation on M3 are
relatively limited as its weight in M3 is only slightly more than
one tenth).

– As a result of a downward-sloping yield curve, investors may shift their
portfolios into short-dated time deposits whenever short-term rates are
higher than long-term rates.

The extent of the yield curve effect remains a matter of debate. The portfolio
reallocations in response to changes in interest rate patterns can occur within the
broad M3 aggregate as well as between time deposits (included in M3) and non-
monetary assets. Indeed, as in former periods of high interest rates, most of the
expansionary effects on short-term time deposits have reflected shifts between
low-interest-bearing short-term savings deposits and high-yielding short-term
time deposits – that is, shifts within M3. That part of short-term time deposit

expansion which may be attributed to shifts out of non-M3 assets actually tended to decline during 1993 and has only marginally contributed to the 1993/94 overshooting.

According to the Bundesbank's analysis, monetary overshooting in 1993 and early 1994 has mainly been the result of special factors, and the long-term relationship with nominal income is not in doubt (see Annex I). However, while the Bundesbank has largely discounted these special factors and clearly indicated that above-target M3 does not rule out further monetary easing, there is a risk that continuous overshooting could either jeopardise the credibility of monetary policy or lead to too high long-term interest rates. Indeed, given the on-going process of innovation and internationalisation in financial markets, money demand may have become persistently more volatile, though there is no clear evidence of this. Consequently, the policy emphasis on monetary targeting needs to be qualified by reference to other leading indicators of inflation. Official emphasis on a wider range of indicators of inflationary pressures, such as wage and price developments, exchange rate stability, or the level and structure of interest rates would be consistent with the Bundesbank's recent behaviour and should help to avoid the reputation problem generated by increased money demand volatility.

Credit demand, long-term rates and the yield curve

As evidenced by the counterparts of M3, bank lending has been the driving force of monetary expansion (Table 11). Public sector borrowing (public authorities plus public enterprises) has recently accounted for about two-fifths of total bank lending, a weight attributable to a deterioration in the financial position of local governments and of public corporations, including the Treuhand agency, in the face of unexpected revenue shortfalls. Bank lending has also been driven by the increased demand for housing, especially in eastern Germany, bolstered towards the end of the year by the anticipated reduction, as from January 1994, of tax concessions available on the acquisition of owner-occupied old buildings. By contrast, business credit demand has been sluggish, reflecting weakness in invest-ment spending. However, the spread between the interest rate on loans of DM 1 to 5 million, which constitutes an overdraft facility, and the day-to-day rate has widened somewhat since 1992, indicating that monetary easing may have been partly absorbed by increased bank margins (Diagram 11, panel B). While the cuts

Table 11. **Lending by credit institutions**

DM billion

	1991	1992	1993
Lending to domestic enterprises and individuals	+244.5	+223.1	+203.1
Lending excluding housing loans	+192.2	+147.3	+88.0
To domestic enterprises and self-employed persons	+156.1	+118.1	+64.4
To individuals and non-profit organisations	+36.1	+28.9	+23.7
Housing loans	+52.3	+76.0	+115.1
Lending to domestic public authorities	+36.0	+17.2	+51.1
of which:			
Länder and local authorities	+30.2	+21.8	+43.5

Source: Deutsche Bundesbank, *Monthly Report.*

in the minimum reserve requirement affecting the banks' term deposits and savings accounts (in March 1993) and sight deposits (in March 1994) constitute a considerable cost saving for the banks as a whole, and should foster their ability to pass on cheaper credit to consumers, the spread has not yet stabilised.

During the present cycle, the downward slope of the yield curve has flattened since the beginning of 1993 – half a year after the first cuts in official interest rates (Diagram 13). This was mainly due to the fact that – contrary to the previous recession – long-term interest rates, in accordance with international interest rate trends, were decreasing at nearly the same pace as short-term rates in the initial stages of the monetary easing (Diagram 14). The normalisation of the term structure in the course of 1994 has not only been the result of further interest rate cuts by the Bundesbank but also of increasing long-term bond rates, pushed upwards by tensions in international capital markets, connected with the strength of the recovery of business activity and inflation fears in the United States.

Recent interest rate patterns should be seen in the perspective of a relatively low exposure of German business to short-term interest rates. Only about one fourth of corporate bank borrowing is short-term and this has alleviated pressures for monetary easing. Nevertheless, although this is a fairly small fraction, short-term interest rates are relevant for some important sectors, notably manufacturing, where the share of short-term credit – mainly for financing stocks – amounts to around 40 per cent. Moreover, it appears that roughly one third of long-term loans are at variable interest rates, which raises the cyclical sensitivity of borrow-

50

Diagram 13. LONG-TERM BOND YIELDS AND THE YIELD STRUCTURE

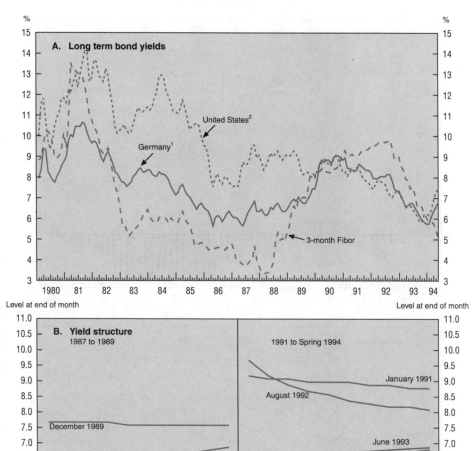

1. 7-15 years German public sector bonds.
2. US Goverment bonds, composite over 10 years.
Source: Deutsche Bundesbank and OECD, *Main Economic Indicators.*

51

Diagram 14. **MONETARY CONDITIONS**

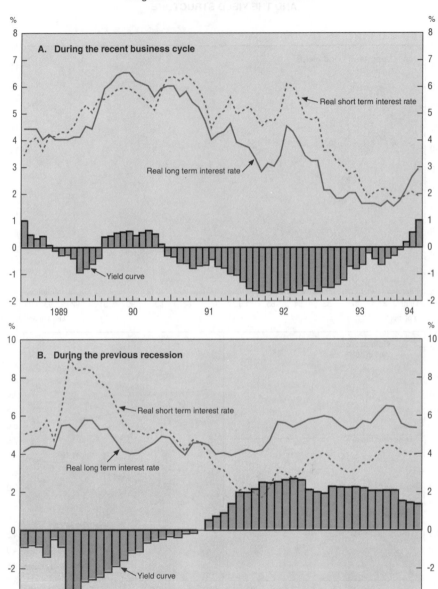

Source: OECD.

Diagram 15. **GDP GROWTH AND THE YIELD STRUCTURE**

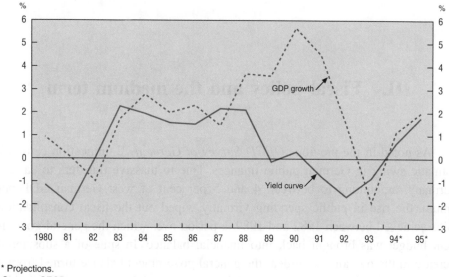

GDP growth

Yield curve

* Projections.
Source: OECD.

ing costs. Furthermore, while there is general agreement that in Germany the major financial determinant of investment are long-term rates – relative to the expected rate of return on physical capital – it has been argued that an inverted yield-curve may attract investors into short-term financial assets and thus lead to postponement of real business capital formation. The net gains from such a strategy may be negligible or even negative when set against the costs of deferred rationalisation investment in terms of losses of competitiveness. Indeed, econometric evidence shows profitability to be the most powerful explanatory variable for the level of investment.[16] But short-term interest rates do have cash-flow effects and thus may have an impact on investment. Overall, judging from historical experience, lower short-term *and* long-term interest rates, associated with an upward-sloping yield curve, would appear to be best suited to bolster the recovery and the OECD projections incorporate such a development (Diagram 15).

III. Fiscal policy and the medium term

As noted in the previous *OECD Survey of Germany*,[17] unification caused a dramatic swing in German public finances. Due to massive transfers to eastern Germany, amounting to between 4 and 5 per cent of west German GDP per annum, the rise in public spending virtually wiped out the fiscal consolidation gains achieved between 1982 and 1989, a period over which the general government budget was brought back into financial balance. In spite of a substantial increase in the overall tax burden, the general government balance turned from a small surplus in 1989 into a deficit of 2.6 per cent of GDP in 1992 (Diagram 16). Given the magnitude of the unification shock, a temporary fiscal deterioration could indeed be seen as appropriate. However, adjustment problems in eastern Germany proved more severe than originally expected, and the situation was aggravated when the western German economy entered recession. In 1993, as the German economy reached the trough of the recession, the deficit increased to 3.3 per cent. Although significantly below the OECD average, a sustained deficit of this magnitude would exceed the level required to stabilise the government debt to GDP ratio. Moreover, the public sector borrowing requirement, which also includes the net credit demand by the Treuhandanstalt and the public enterprises, increased to 5.2 per cent of GDP, equivalent to about half of domestic saving.

Due to increases in social security contributions, value-added tax and other indirect taxes, as well as expenditure cuts, the *structural* deficit has already been reduced from 5 per cent in 1991 to 3 per cent in 1993. This is near to the OECD average and the government is now embarked on a medium-term strategy to reduce it further, while rolling back the public sector to pre-unification levels by the end of the decade. In the short-term the strategy relies heavily on higher taxes and social security charges to reduce the deficit. In the medium term, it is based on expenditure restraint, with current spending of territorial authorities allowed to

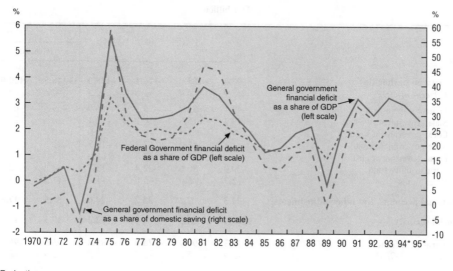

Diagram 16. **PUBLIC SECTOR FINANCIAL BALANCES**

General government
financial deficit
as a share of GDP
(left scale)

Federal Government financial deficit
as a share of GDP (left scale)

General government financial deficit
as a share of domestic saving (right scale)

1970 71 72 73 74 75 76 77 78 79 80 81 82 83 84 85 86 87 88 89 90 91 92 93 94* 95*

* Projections.
Source: OECD.

increase by no more than 3 per cent a year in nominal terms – slightly more than half the projected increase in nominal GDP. The resources thereby freed would be used, among other things, for growth-promoting tax-relief and investment spending in eastern Germany. Meanwhile, fiscal consolidation is also paving the way for a more balanced policy mix. Fiscal slippage has placed monetary policy under some strain over the past few years, and expenditure restraint could be expected to relieve this.

Public finances in 1993 and 1994

The 1993 budget

The deficit of the territorial authorities[18] expanded by about DM 22 billion to approximately DM 138 billion (4.4 per cent of GDP) in 1993 (Table 12). The widening was largely attributable to the federal budget, which absorbed most of the pressure arising from reunification and the recession. The federal deficit

Table 12. **Public sector financial balances**

DM billion

	1990	1991	1992	1993	1994	1995
					Projected	
Territorial authorities	**−94.4**	**−123.0**	**−116.1**	**−138.0**	**−146.5**	**−130.0**
Per cent of GDP	*−3.9*	*−4.4*	*−3.8*	*−4.5*	*−4½*	*−4*
Federal government	−48.1	−53.2	−39.3	−66.9	−69¾	−69½
State government west[1]	−19.4	−15.8	−16.2	−22.1	−28	−29½
Local government west	−4.2	−5.5	−9.7	−9.0	−9	−8
State government east[1]	..	−13.4	−15.3	−19.7	−22	−9½
Local government east	..	1.5	−7.4	−5.0	−3	−2
German unity fund	−20.0	−30.6	−22.4	−13.5	−3	2
Other funds[2]	−2.7	−6.0	−5.8	−1.8	−11½	−13
National accounts and other adjustments[3]	**24.3**	**7.3**	**33.2**	**24.0**	**33.5**	**17.8**
Social security	**20.4**	**24.8**	**4.4**	**12.2**	**17.5**	**15.5**
General government	**−49.7**	**−90.9**	**−78.5**	**−101.8**	**−95.5**	**−96.7**
Per cent of GDP	*−2.0*	*−3.2*	*−2.6*	*−3.3*	*−2.9*	*−2.8*
Memorandum items:						
Treuhandanstalt	−4.3	−19.9	−29.7	−38.1	−41.0	..
Public enterprises[4]	−9.9	−15.6	−25.7	−20.5	−11.3	10.0
Public sector, broadly defined	**−63.9**	**−138.3**	**−136.0**	**−160.4**	**−147.8**	**−106.7**
Per cent of GDP	*−2.6*	*−4.9*	*−4.5*	*−5.2*	*−4.6*	*−3.2*
Per cent of domestic saving	*21.1*	*50.0*	*49.4*	*47.7*		

1. 1991-93; west without Berlin; east including Berlin.
2. Credit fund, Economic Recovery Programme fund, financial equalisation fund, railway fund and inherited debt fund.
3. Lending operations, dividend paid by the Bundesbank and timing and data adjustments.
4. Post/Telecom and Railway Companies in the West and in the East; projections for Post/Telecom only.
Source: Ministry of Finance, Finanzbericht 1994; Deutsche Bundesbank, *Monthly Report*; Ministry of Finance submissions and Federal Consolidation Programme; OECD projections.

turned out to be DM 66.9 billion, compared with the initial estimate of DM 43 billion (Table 13). As the slowdown turned out to be sharper than expected, the authorities allowed the "automatic stabilisers" to operate, no measures being taken to offset cyclically-related tax shortfalls and spending overruns. The growth of federal tax receipts, at less than 1 per cent, was actually inferior to the 2.6 per cent increase in nominal GDP, whereas federal expenditures grew by about 7.1 per cent. Higher transfers to the Federal Labour Office (DM 24.4 billion compared with DM 8.9 billion in 1992) accounted for about half of the spending increase.

Table 13. **The Federal Budget**

DM billion

	1989	1990	1991	1992	1993	1994
Expenditure	**289.8**	**380.2**	**401.8**	**427.2**	**457.5**	**480.0**
(As a per cent of GDP)	(13.0)	(15.7)	(14.3)	(14.1)	(14.7)	(14.9)
of which:						
Consumption	82.2	85.6	91.8	95.5	94.5	93.5
Interest payments	32.1	34.2	39.6	43.8	45.8	52.8
Investment	8.0	8.5	11.0	13.8	12.5	13.2
Transfers and lending	167.5	252.0	259.4	274.1	304.7	320.5
of which:						
To other administrations	37.6	40.5	64.9	78.0	81.9	101.9
Others	129.9	211.5	194.5	196.0	222.8	218.6
Revenues	**269.7**	**332.1**	**348.6**	**387.8**	**390.5**	**410.3**
(As a per cent of GDP)	(12.1)	(13.7)	(12.4)	(12.8)	(12.6)	(12.7)
of which:						
Taxes	247.1	276.0	317.9	352.9	356.0	375.2
Others	22.6	56.0	30.7	34.9	34.5	35.1
Financial balance	**–20.1**	**–48.0**	**–53.2**	**–39.3**	**–66.9**	**–69.7**
As a per cent of GDP	–0.9	–2.0	–1.9	–1.3	–2.2	–2.1

Source: Ministry of Finance, *Finanzbericht 1994* and submission.

The spending of the federal states ("Länder") grew by 5.4 per cent, driven mainly by public sector wage increases, a general increase of 3 per cent being amplified by the fact that eastern wages were raised from 74 to 80 per cent of the western level as from 1 July. In the local authority sector, expenditure grew by 4½ per cent, pushed up by a sharp rise in social assistance payments associated both with the shedding of labour and the influx of persons seeking political asylum. With receipts undershooting initial estimates, the combined deficit of Länder and municipalities widened from DM 48.9 to DM 55.8 billion.

This deterioration was partly offset at the level of general government by a higher social security surplus, which rose from DM 4.4 billion to DM 12.2 billion, an improvement which can be traced to better control on health spending and higher contribution rates in the old Länder. Overall, if the deficits of the Treuhand agency are included, together with those of the Federal Railways and the Federal Post Office, the aggregate borrowing requirement of the public sector edged up to DM 160 billion, or 5.2 per cent of GDP (Table 12).

The 1994 budget

In 1993, as part of the federal government's commitment to the Solidarity Pact, a fiscal retrenchment programme (the "Federal Consolidation Programme") was adopted, which had the aim of halting the deterioration in government finances due to unification (see previous *OECD Economic Survey of Germany*). Most of the provisions, including the "solidarity" surcharge of 7.5 per cent on income tax liabilities (worth DM 26 billion) are due to take effect only as of 1995. However, the government introduced a second package of corrective measures in the 1994 budget (the "Savings Consolidation and Growth Programme") intended to rein in the deficit this year.[19] The programmed savings, amounting to DM 21 billion (or 0.6 per cent of GDP), are principally composed of social spending reductions (DM 15 billion), affecting in particular unemployment compensation and assistance (Table 14), a zero wage round for civil servants and a more than 1 per cent decline in staff. Measures are also being

Table 14.   **New measures in the 1994 federal budget**

DM billion

	1993	1994
Baseline balance		**–87.9**
New measures		
New expenditures		17.0
Railways reform		11.8
Higher contribution to the German Unity Fund		5.2
Expenditure cuts		27.3
of which:		
Cuts included in the Savings Consolidation and Growth Programme		19.0
Measures to combat tax and social security fraud (included in the Savings Consolidation and Growth Programme)		1.9
Higher mineral oil tax		7.9
Financial balance	**–66.9**	**–69.7**
Primary balance	**–21.1**	**–16.9**

Source: Ministry of Finance.

taken to combat tax and social security fraud. Overall, federal outlays are expected to rise by 5 per cent, almost half of which stems from a reform of the railways, as a result of which the federal government has assumed responsibility for the debt accumulated by that sector (DM 66 billion). The cost of the reform is partly covered by an increase in the mineral oil tax (expected to yield DM 8 billion). Against this background, and assuming a GDP growth of 1.5 per cent and an inflation of 3 per cent, the official objective is to limit the federal deficit to DM 70 billion, just above its 1993 level. Further savings, accounting for DM 7.5 billion (and concerning, in particular, defence and transport appropriations) are to be implemented in the course of the year (of which DM 5 billion have already been approved).

The beginning of 1994 also saw the implementation of an already announced business tax reform designed to improve Germany's attractiveness as a business location, which reduced the tax burden on businesses by DM 4 billion. The fiscal consolidation measures should also help to restore business and household confidence in part by relieving some of the pressure on interest rates. Nevertheless, the 1994 federal budget is likely to have a negative short-run impact on consumer spending. Together with the 1.7 percentage point rise in the old-age insurance contribution rate (yielding DM 22 billion, of which half will be raised from households), the new federal measures would induce a reduction in the general government structural deficit equal to 0.8 per cent of GDP (Table 15).

Table 15. **Indicators of fiscal stance**

Per cent of GDP

	1993	1994
General government financial balance		
Financial balance	–3.3	–2.9
Primary balance	0.0	0.9
Change in cyclically-adjusted balance[1]		**+0.8**
of which:		
Railways reform (deficit)		–0.2
Savings consolidation and growth programme		+0.8
Other federal expenditure cuts		+0.3
Rise in contributions to the pension insurance scheme		+0.7

1. A positive sign indicates a lower deficit.
Source: Ministry of Finance; OECD estimates.

The effect on aggregate demand depends on how consumers adjust their saving (see below), but the "first-round" impact amounts to a withdrawal of demand stimulus equal to around 2 per cent of household disposable income.

Transfers to the new Länder

In the wake of reunification, the government embarked on a massive programme of consumption transfers and infrastructure investment in eastern Germany. In 1993, total public transfers to the new Länder, net of federal tax receipts, amounted to an estimated DM 130 billion, the equivalent of about half of eastern German and 4.6 per cent of western German GDP (Table 16). The lion's share of the gross transfers was already being financed from federal government resources (DM 116 billion out of DM 169 billion in 1993, compared with a DM 10 billion contribution from the western Länder). The issue of bonds by the Unity Fund has also been a significant source of finance, but this Fund,

Table 16. **Public sector transfers to eastern Germany**

DM billion

	1991	1992	1993	1994
1. Gross transfers	**140**	**152**	**169**	**178**
Federal government transfers to the eastern Länder and Communities	75	89	116	127
Western Länder and Communities	5	5	10	14
German Unity Fund borrowing	31	24	15	5
Transfers from EC	4	5	5	6
Other	25	29	23	26
2. Receipts	**33**	**37**	**39**	**42**
of which:				
Federal tax receipts from the east	31	35	37	40
Federal administrative receipts from the east	2	2	2	2
3. Net transfers (1 – 2)	**107**	**115**	**130**	**136**
As a percentage of:				
All-German GDP	3.8	3.8	4.2	4.2
Western German GDP	4.1	4.1	4.6	4.7
Eastern German GDP	58	49	47	44

Source: Estimation by the Ministry of Finance.

created to finance the deficit of the new Länder and municipalities, will be abolished as of 1 January 1995. As of then, the new Länder will be incorporated in the regular revenue-sharing system (designed to avoid unduly large differences in per capita tax yields among the Länder). However, under the Solidarity Pact agreement signed in March 1993, much of the intergovernmental transfer burden will in fact be carried by the federal government. This is because, to help the western Länder to fulfil their obligations under the rules of revenue-sharing among the Länder, the federal government has agreed that the share of VAT going to the Länder will be increased from 37 to 44 per cent as of 1995. In addition, the federal government will continue to provide special transfers to the eastern German Länder. Overall, such federal inter-governmental transfers to the eastern Länder will be as much as DM 41.8 billion, compared with DM 15.6 billion in transfers from the old Länder.

The costs of adjusting eastern German living standards to those in the west have proved to be considerably higher than initially anticipated. With the deepening in labour market slack, an increasing amount of resources have been devoted to job-preserving or job-creating measures and to the support of the unemployed. In addition, the progressive convergence of eastern German social entitlements to western German levels has placed continued upward pressure on the amount of resources to be transferred eastwards. Pensions, in particular, were increased by 21 per cent in the second half of 1993, so that the basic eastern German pension corresponds to 73 per cent of the basic pension in the west. Indeed, as noted in Part I, contrary to initial intentions, the bulk (four-fifths) of financial transfers has been devoted to consumption rather than investment purposes.

Fiscal consolidation

Controlling government debt accumulation

According to OECD estimates, the structural component of the general government deficit amounted to around 3 per cent of GDP in 1993 (Table 17). This represented a marked deterioration over the immediate pre-unification period, when the structural deficit had been negligible. But it also reflects a significant underlying improvement in the structural budget situation over the last two years, when the national accounts deficit has been relatively stable relative to

Table 17. **Structural deficit of the general government**

Per cent of GDP

	1991	1992	1993	1994	1995
Current receipts	45.3	46.4	46.7	47.1	47.7
Expenditures	48.5	49.0	50.0	50.1	50.5
Net lending	−3.2	−2.6	−3.3	−2.9	−2.8
Cyclical component	2.0	1.9	−0.2	−0.6	−0.6
Structural deficit [1]	−5.2	−4.5	−3.1	−2.3	−2.2
Change in general government balance:					
Actual balance		+0.6	−0.7	+0.4	+0.1
Cyclically-adjusted balance		+0.7	+1.4	+0.8	+0.1
Cyclical balance		−0.1	−2.1	−0.4	0.0

1. Net lending minus cyclical component.
Source: OECD estimates.

GDP, despite the recession. This improvement is attributable to increases in social security contributions and taxes, with cyclically-adjusted receipts rising by 1 per cent of GDP between 1991 and 1993, as well as to a 1.4 per cent of GDP decrease in cyclically-adjusted non-interest spending. The consolidation measures described above are thus being implemented against an already improving budgetary trend, and are projected to take the structural deficit down to 1½ per cent of GDP in 1995. On current policies, the structural deficit is projected to remain at this level for the rest of the decade.

Viewed in this perspective, the fiscal consolidation process in Germany appears to be better-established than in the majority of OECD economies. However, two important concerns will remain:

– While, by the end of the decade, the general government debt-to-GDP ratio will be on a downward trend, it will rise in the short term. Thus, in addition to the debt accumulation resulting from general government borrowing, the public debt ratio will be boosted in 1995 by the transfer to the federal government of the accumulated debt related to unification. A considerable part of the reconstruction of eastern Germany has been financed off-budget. A redemption fund will be established, which will assume the debt issued by the Treuhandanstalt and the Credit Fund – which has, among other items, taken over the debt of the former DDR government – as well as part of the debt of the eastern German public housing sector (DM 31 billion). The general government debt ratio will then have breached the ceiling of 60 per cent laid down in the Maastricht Treaty.

– The tax-to-GDP ratio will, on average, be higher than at the beginning of the decade, in part because of the need to service a higher level of government debt, and also because of continuing current transfers.

Although the increase in public debt may be justified in the light of the potential long-run economic gains to be derived from unification, to the extent that higher indebtedness has financed consumption or non-cost-effective investment, higher debt could be self-sustaining, with continuing costs in terms of efficiency losses and reduced room for fiscal manœuvre. Moreover, the problems of controlling government debt are exacerbated by a number of quasi-exogenous factors, including *i)* real interest rates higher than the growth rate of the economy; *ii)* a build-up of contingent liabilities not recognised in the conventional budget accounts.

Pressure on the debt ratio will increase or diminish according to the gap between the effective real interest rate and the economic growth rate. This gap determines the size of the primary (non-interest) surplus needed to stabilise the debt-to-GDP ratio. In 1993, with the average interest rate on public debt exceeding the growth rate by 4½ percentage points, the primary surplus necessary to keep the general government debt ratio constant would have been about 2¼ per cent of GDP, compared with an actual value of under ½ per cent (Diagram 17). As a result, the general government debt ratio, which had been low by international standards during the 1980s, rose rapidly during the recession (Table 18). This situation will correct itself as the recovery proceeds, but the likelihood is that real interest rates will continue to exceed the growth rate, calling for a primary budget surplus of ½ to 1 per cent just to stabilise the debt-GDP ratio.

The problem of stabilising the debt as a share of GDP is made all the more severe because of potential pressures arising from liabilities not identified in the conventional budget accounts:

– The amount of debt guaranteed by the federal government stood at DM 218 billion in 1993, DM 167 billion of which arose from exports. In the 1994 budget, the cost of these guarantees, on account of defaults,

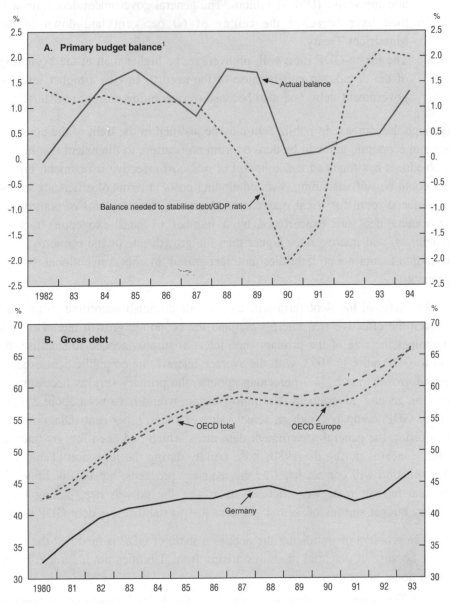

Diagram 17. **PUBLIC DEBT AND THE PRIMARY BUDGET BALANCE**

Per cent of GDP

A. Primary budget balance[1]

Actual balance

Balance needed to stabilise debt/GDP ratio

1982 83 84 85 86 87 88 89 90 91 92 93 94

B. Gross debt

OECD total

OECD Europe

Germany

1980 81 82 83 84 85 86 87 88 89 90 91 92 93

1. Two period moving average of t and t+1.
Source: OECD.

Table 18. **Public debt by government level**
DM billion

	1990	1991	1992	1993
Federal government	542	586	611	685
Länder West	329	347	366	392
Länder East	–	5	23	37
Communities West	126	132	141	136
Communities East	–	9	13	17
Unity fund	20	51	74	88
Credit fund	28	27	92	101
ERP fund	9	16	24	28
Total – General Government [1]	**1 054**	**1 173**	**1 345**	**1 496**
(as a share of GDP)	*43.5*	*41.7*	*44.4*	*48.1*
Treuhandanstalt	14	57	110	169
Post Office	71	81	97	105
Railways	48	43	53	66
Total – Public Sector	**1 187**	**1 354**	**1 605**	**1 836**
(as a share of GDP)	*48.9*	*48.1*	*53.0*	*59.0*

1. Including indebtedness of municipal special-purpose associations and municipal hospitals.
Source: Ministry of Finance.

will amount to DM 7.5 billion. Adverse developments in the transition economies of central and eastern Europe and in developing countries could trigger more substantial debt reschedulings and sizeable payment of claims in the future.

– Germany, like other industrialised countries, will face the problem of supporting a rapidly-ageing population in coming decades. According to OECD estimates for western Germany, in 1990 public pension net liabilities stemming from already-acquired pension rights under current legislation amounted to the equivalent of 150 per cent of GDP – three times the amount of conventional debt.[20]

Fiscal consolidation scenarios

To explore the constraints involved in the setting of German fiscal policy over the coming years, Diagram 18 sets out a range of macroeconomic scenarios for the period 1995-2000. Incorporating the measures decided in the budget consolidation programmes, a reference scenario would base the evolution of

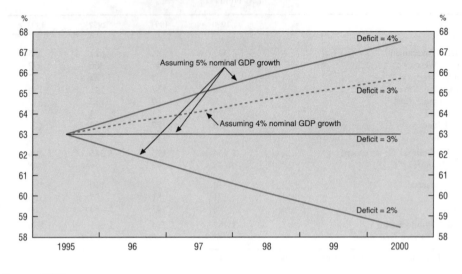

Diagram 18. **MEDIUM-TERM DEBT DEVELOPMENTS UNDER VARIOUS ASSUMPTIONS**

Source: OECD.

public debt on an average budget deficit of around 2 per cent from 1995 to 2000 (see Annex II). The combination of sustained medium-term growth and active programmes of fiscal consolidation would be sufficient to achieve a ratio of general government debt to GDP of around 60 per cent by around the end of the projection period. However, this scenario depends crucially upon a dynamic and self-supporting catching-up in eastern Germany. Moreover, the success of the consolidation process will also depend on Länder and local authorities, whose budgets are one-third larger than the federal budget, pursuing a consistent medium-term policy of consolidation. The previous period of consolidation (1982-1989) was characterised by a below-average expansion of federal outlays (2½ per year on average), while Länder and local authorities' spending grew somewhat faster (3½ per year). For the future, there may be inadequate incentives for expenditure restraint at the eastern Länder and local levels, given, in particular, the likely scenario of rapid wage equalisation. There are also potential demands for higher local authority spending on statutory kindergarten places and new sewage treatment works demanded by European legislation. Länder and municipalities may be inclined to some extent to trim their expenditures to redress their own imbalances, for example by reductions in current overstaffing in the eastern Länder. But, the revised system of revenue-sharing between the federal and the Länder governments leaves much of the west-east transfer burden with the federal government, making it less compelling for Länder and munici- palities to adhere to the 3 per cent expenditure guideline.

The adoption of more conservative deficit and growth assumptions points to the extreme sensitivity of fiscal outcomes to changes in economic conditions (Diagram 18 and Annex II). An assumption of a 3 per cent deficit would imply a stable debt ratio over the medium term, at around 64 per cent. And if this were combined with 4 per cent average nominal income growth, the debt-to-GDP ratio would tend to rise. To offset the slippage resulting from the lower growth assumption, expenditure growth would need to be curbed further.

A number of lessons emerge. First, under present medium-term budget guidelines, a sustained recovery would be sufficient to bring the debt-to-GDP ratio back to around the 60 per cent level laid down in the Maastricht Treaty. Second, current receipts would stand at 45½ per cent of GDP by the end of the decade, 1½ percentage points above the pre-unification levels. This consideration demands both that the scope for expenditure cuts be further evaluated and that measures be taken to create the most favourable conditions for growth. Policy options for improving the foundations for medium-term growth are examined in the next chapter.

IV. Improving the foundations for growth

Introduction

While the problems of inflation and the budget deficit are on course for correction, the possibilities that the recession might be partly structural in origin, and problems of competitiveness and unemployment more entrenched, have generated renewed debate about the long-run attractiveness of Germany as an investment and production location. If it were the case that Germany's problems derived mainly from cyclical demand insufficiency, then attributing them to structural factors could lead to inappropriate structural policy responses.[21] But an equal danger derives from the possibility that the unification boom may have covered up serious structural defects which have now been unmasked by recession; in this case it would be even more misleading to expect them to be corrected by, for example, an expansionary monetary policy.[22] At stake in the current debate – which represents a revival of the early 1980s *Standort* controversy – is the longer-run effectiveness of the German economic model, the "Social Market economy". This model has traditionally been based on a balance of market freedom and social consensus and has been considered a major element in Germany's competitive strength. It may now be endangered by the spiralling costs of maintaining a large-scale government presence in the economy, both directly, in terms of non-wage costs, and indirectly via the widespread diversion of economic activity into rent-seeking behaviour.

The debate has revolved, *inter alia,* around the possibility of structural problems existing in three main areas:

- *Excessive costs*, arising from unit wage pressures, social charges and taxes, and insufficient competition, which could permanently undermine the competitiveness of German products.

– *Lagging technological innovation,* reflecting regulatory barriers and lack of efficient risk financing, which inhibit the establishment of new firms, especially those proposing new technologies.
– The possibility that the German *education and training* system may be insufficiently adapted to the needs of structural change.

Each of these problem areas pose threats to German growth potential, which will need to be overcome if the challenges of unification, the opening of eastern Europe and rapid population ageing are to be successfully met. Hence, a thorough re-examination of the framework conditions for growth is appropriate. The first section of this chapter analyses the extent to which Germany's supply-side performance has deteriorated. The second identifies the major structural and institutional deficiencies underlying such deterioration, where it has occurred, while the final part assesses the adequacy of recent structural policy initiatives and proposes an agenda for further reform.[23]

Growth, employment and competitiveness

Slowing output growth and rising structural unemployment

Germany has not been immune from the OECD-wide trend towards slower growth and higher unemployment. Over the past 20 years, growth rates have declined with each new business cycle. The rate of growth of real GDP, as measured between cyclical peaks, halved after the first oil shock and edged down again in the post-OPEC II period. Moreover, while potential output growth declined, the average level of cyclical slack grew larger with each cycle (Diagram 19), indicating a tendency to slower cyclical adjustment (Table 19). If these characteristics persist, German growth performance could remain unsatisfactory, though rapid growth in the eastern Länder will help to compensate for slow growth in the west.

The growth slowdown has been associated with a weakening trend of net capital formation. The growth of the business sector capital stock slowed from 6 per cent in 1960-73 to around 3½ per cent in 1973-79, and to less than 3 per cent in 1980-91, being projected to remain around this level in the medium-term (Table 20). This slowdown was, on average, more severe than in the United States, but less severe than in other OECD Europe (Diagram 20, panel A). It was

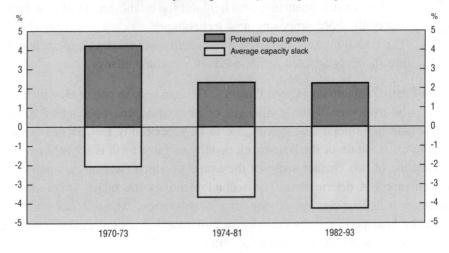

Diagram 19. **POTENTIAL OUTPUT AND CAPACITY SLACK**

West Germany; average annual percentage change

Legend:
- Potential output growth
- Average capacity slack

Source: Sachverständigenrat zur Begutachtung der gesamtwirtschaftlichen Entwicklung, *Jahresgutachten,* 1993/94.

Table 19. **Growth performance in the major seven OECD countries**[1]

	1950-59	1960-73	1974-79	1980-91	1992-2000 Projection
Western Germany[2]	8.2	4.4	2.4	2.3	1.7[3]
France	4.6	5.6	2.8	2.2	2.3
Italy	5.6	5.3	3.7	2.3	2.0
United Kingdom	2.8	3.3	1.5	1.9	2.2
United States	3.3	3.9	2.6	2.1	2.6
Japan	8.8	9.6	3.6	4.1	2.6
Canada	4.0[4]	5.3	4.2	2.4	3.3

1. Average annual growth rates of gross domestic product (for the United States and Japan, prior to 1960, gross national product) at constant prices.
2. For 1950-59 excluding the Saar and Berlin.
3. Growth rate for unified Germany is 2.3 per cent.
4. 1955-59.
Source: 1950-59: Giersch *et al., The fading miracle: four decades of market economy in Germany,* Cambridge University Press, 1992; 1960-2000: OECD.

Table 20. **Business sector output, factor inputs and productivity**

Western Germany; average annual percent changes

	1950-59[1]	1960-73	1974-79	1980-91	1992-95 Projection
Output	8.2	4.5	2.3	2.5	0.9
Labour volume	0.9	-1.1	-1.7	0.0	-0.6
Number of employed persons	3.3	-0.1	-0.7	0.8	-0.7
Average hours per worker	-2.4	-1.0	-1.0	-0.8	0.1
Capital stock	4.8	6.0	3.4	2.8	2.7
Labour productivity	7.3	5.6	4.0	2.5	1.5
due to :					
Increased capital/labour ratio[2]	1.2	2.3	1.7	0.9	1.1
Total factor productivity[3]	6.9	3.3	2.4	1.6	0.5
Memorandum items:					
Nominal wage growth[4]	..	11.1	8.0	5.5	2.4
Real product wage growth[5]	..	6.7	3.1	2.4	-0.5
Real long-term interest rate[6]	4.0	2.8	3.1	4.6	3.6

1. Data for 1950-59 refer to gross domestic product at constant prices and total-economy inputs.
2. Capital/labour ratio times long-run average capital income share (also equals labour productivity minus total factor productivity).
3. Output growth minus a weighted average of capital and labour input growth, using long-run average factor shares in national income as weights.
4. Hourly nominal wage including employer's contribution to social security.
5. Nominal wage growth less GDP deflator inflation.
6. 7 to 15-year government bond yield less GDP deflator inflation; proxy for opportunity cost of fixed capital.

Source: 1950-59: Giersch *et al., op. cit.;* 1960-95: OECD.

associated with a steep fall in profitability up to the early 1980s (Diagram 21). During the latter half of the 1980s, however, profitability recovered strongly, due largely to wage moderation and terms-of-trade gains. This in turn evoked a record investment boom in the 1987-91 period despite a doubling of real interest rates. The fact that the trend rate of capital stock growth failed to recover reflected the simultaneously high rate of scrapping as the capital stock was modernised. A significant part of capital stock growth was labour-substituting rather than capacity-creating, moreover, as labour input tended to decline more in Germany than elsewhere, due to shorter working hours, longer holidays and earlier retirements (Diagram 20, panel B).[24]

Labour productivity growth has also slowed sharply. Splitting productivity growth (measured by value added per hour) into its capital-intensity and residual components shows that, although the deceleration in growth of the capital stock

Diagram 20. **FACTOR INPUT GROWTH
IN THE BUSINESS SECTOR**
Annual averages

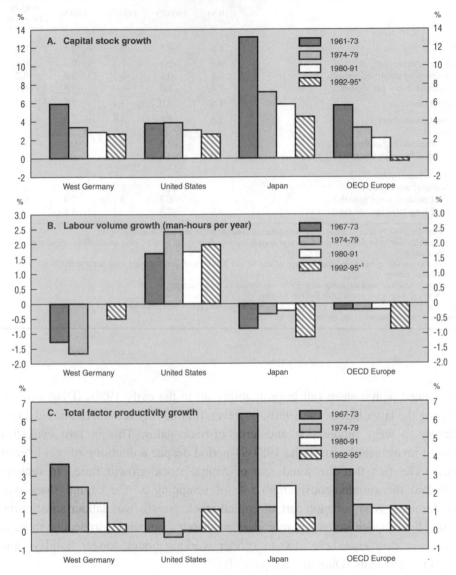

* 1994 and 1995 projected.
1. Employment in the private sector; total employment for OECD Europe.
Source: OECD.

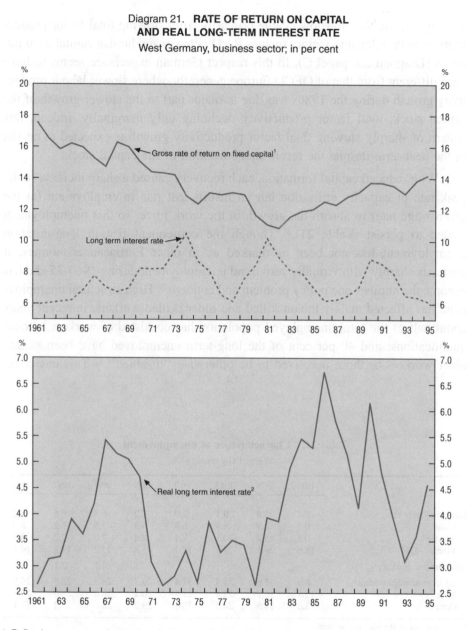

Diagram 21. **RATE OF RETURN ON CAPITAL
AND REAL LONG-TERM INTEREST RATE**

West Germany, business sector; in per cent

Gross rate of return on fixed capital[1]

Long term interest rate

Real long term interest rate[2]

1. Defined as gross operating surplus of enterprises (value added at factor cost minus labour income) as a
   percentage of the capital stock.
2. 7-15 year public sector bond yield less the rate of consumer price inflation.
Source: OECD, *National Accounts.*

was significant, the slowdown came primarily from slowing total factor productivity growth, related to factors such as R&D potency and human capital accumulation (Diagram 20, panel C). In this respect German experience seems to have been different from that of OECD Europe generally, where slower labour productivity growth during the 1980s was due in major part to the slower growth of the capital stock, total factor productivity declining only marginally. Indeed, this pattern of sharply slowing total factor productivity growth is expected to persist in the near-term despite the recent modernisation of the capital stock.

With reduced capital formation, each recovery caused a sharp increase in the peak rate of capacity utilisation but an insufficient rise in employment (at the given wage rate) to absorb the growth in the work force, so that unemployment tended to persist (Table 21).[25] Though the consequent rise in long-duration unemployment has not been as marked as in other European economies, it contrasts sharply with virtually zero trend unemployment during 1960-75 and has become the number one policy problem and concern.[26] High structural unemployment has affected mainly the unskilled and older skilled workers: in recent years about half of the total unemployed population has consisted of workers without qualifications; and 40 per cent of the long-term unemployed have been skilled older workers or those perceived to be otherwise "disabled".[27] This has coex-

Table 21. **Characteristics of unemployment**

Western Germany

	1970	1979	1983	1989	1990	1991	1992	1993
Unemployment rate, total[1]	0.7	3.8	9.1	7.9	7.2	6.3	6.6	8.2
Male[2]	0.7	2.9	8.4	6.9	6.3	5.8	6.2	8.0
Female[2]	0.8	5.2	10.1	9.4	8.4	7.0	7.2	8.5
Youth (−25)[3]	18.6	26.1	29.2	17.3	15.8	15.2	14.8	14.1
Discouraged workers[1]	..	..	..	..	..	2.1	2.1	2.7
Long term unemployment[4]	8.9	15.6	24.9	31.4	29.7	28.3	26.6	26.0
Male	15.7	16.9	25.4	32.4	30.2	28.0	26.0	25.1
Female	2.0	14.5	24.2	30.4	29.2	28.6	27.2	27.1

1. In per cent of the total labour force.
2. In per cent of the labour force in the relevant groups.
3. In per cent of total unemployment.
4. Twelve months and over, as a per cent of numbers unemployed in the relevant groups (in September).
Source: Bundesanstalt für Arbeit; United States: Bureau of Labor Statistics, *Employment and Earnings.*

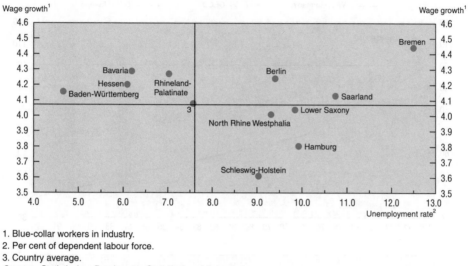

Diagram 22. **REGIONAL UNEMPLOYMENT RATES AND WAGE GROWTH**
Average in 1980-92, per cent

1. Blue-collar workers in industry.
2. Per cent of dependent labour force.
3. Country average.
Source: Statistisches Bundesamt, *Statistisches Jahrbuch.*

isted with chronic shortages of skilled labour in high-growth sectors and regions, which may have impeded growth performance.[28]

A marked dispersion in regional unemployment rates may also be observed (Diagram 22). In the context of a rather narrow regional dispersion of wage increases, this suggests a high degree of inter-sectoral wage rigidity in addition to low geographical mobility of labour. The regional distribution of unemployment has furthermore tended to reflect the sectoral problems caused by structural change-modern services and high-tech manufacturing being characteristic of such low-unemployment states as Baden-Württemberg, while high unemployment rates are found in traditional heavy-industry and mining areas such as Saarland and North Rhine Westphalia.

Structural change

In broad terms, the OECD has experienced a sustained shrinkage of agricultural and (since 1973) manufacturing sectors in favour of a rapidly developing service sector (Diagram 23). Germany has shared in these trends, but the shift of

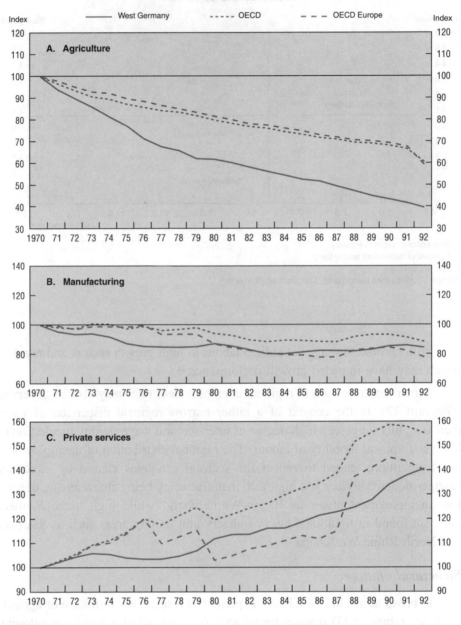

Diagram 23. **SECTORAL EMPLOYMENT TRENDS**

1970 = 100

West Germany ——— OECD ····· OECD Europe – – –

A. Agriculture

B. Manufacturing

C. Private services

Source: OECD, *Labour force statistics.*

production and employment out of manufacturing has been less marked than elsewhere, with manufacturing and exports moreover remaining based on traditional, mainly investment goods, production. At present, 30 per cent of the labour force in Germany is still employed in manufacturing against only 17 per cent in the United States and 19 per cent in the OECD on average. Indeed, Germany is a striking exception to the general rule that manufacturing employment makes up a lower share of employment in those countries with a higher per capita GDP. Likewise, the manufacturing share of output is higher in Germany than anywhere else in the EC.[29] Such developments suggest a persisting comparative advantage in manufacturing.[30]

On the other hand, this relatively good manufacturing output and employment performance has been accompanied by slow and decelerating productivity growth which has eroded Germany's advantage in terms of internationally high *levels* of productivity. Manufacturing productivity on a per capita basis grew by 1.3 per cent in the 1980-90 period, compared with 2.9 per cent for the EC and 4.2 per cent in the United States. Moreover, this reflected a significant deceleration, whereas elsewhere in the OECD area manufacturing productivity accelerated. However, the shortfall compared to the EC largely reflected the sharp cuts in hours worked in Germany, so that on a per-hour basis the lag in manufacturing productivity growth occurred mainly *vis-à-vis* the United States and Japan (see below).

At the same time, Germany's productivity growth in the market services sector has slightly exceeded that of the EC and substantially bettered that of the United States (Table 22). This helped Germany to enjoy a relatively low rate of inflation in such services; the rate of price increase was, unusually, slightly lower than in manufacturing during the decade prior to unification. And the *level* of service sector productivity has also been relatively favourable compared with the EC average (although still considerably below that of the United States), perhaps reflecting the compositional benefits of concentrating activity in areas such as transport, banking and business services, where productivity gains have generally been high. Nevertheless, the trend in services has been (like manufacturing) towards a deceleration in productivity growth, whereas such growth, though slower, has been steadier in the rest of the OECD. Moreover, investment in services has grown no faster than the rather slow EC average and much slower than in the United States, Japan and the United Kingdom.[31] Although inter-

Table 22.   **Weight of market services in the German economy** [1]

	Germany	Europe	United States
	Per cent		
A. Output and employment			
Weight of services in GDP	45.9	48.2	54.1
Change 1980-1990	4.8	5.8	4.8
Weight of services in employment	38.0	42.0	51.7
Change 1980-1990	4.3	5.6	4.9
B. International trade			
Weight of non-factor services in total trade			
Exports	15.0	22.3	25.4
Imports	21.1	20.4	18.4
	Average annual percentage change		
C. Labour productivity growth 1980-1990			
Services	1.4	1.2	0.4
Manufacturing	1.3	2.9	4.2
D. Inflation: difference between services			
and manufacturing	**–0.5**	**1.1**	**3.3**

1.   In 1990.
Source: European Economy (1993), *op. cit.;* Bundesbank calculations.

sectoral real labour cost developments generally favoured a shift of investment towards services, the inter-sectoral wage structure was nevertheless marked by a fair amount of rigidity (Table 23). As a result, the overall gain in service output has been comparatively small and the corresponding increase in service-sector employment since 1973 has been limited to about 3¹/₃ million (40 per cent growth),[32] against a net loss of 2 million in industry (Diagram 24). Furthermore, the level of non-factor service exports as a proportion of total exports of goods and services – at 15 per cent – is far lower than both the EC and United States averages of close to 25 per cent.

International competitiveness

Over the long-term, Germany has been losing its already small export market shares outside the EC while consolidating its strong lead within Europe (Table 24). Since unification, however, it has lost market shares globally. This

Table 23. **Determinants of labour costs in manufacturing and the service sector** [1]

Western Germany; average annual percentage change

	1960-73	1974-79	1980-91	1992
Value added deflator				
Manufacturing	2.9	4.0	3.1	3.2
Services	4.9	4.8	3.1	5.4
Labour productivity [2]				
Manufacturing	4.8	3.4	1.3	0.2
Services	3.4	2.4	1.7	−0.2
Nominal wages [3]				
Manufacturing	9.2	8.4	4.7	5.8
Services	9.2	6.9	3.9	5.2
Real unit labour cost [4]				
Manufacturing	1.3	0.8	0.3	2.4
Services	0.7	−0.3	−0.9	0.0
Memorandum items:				
Employment				
Manufacturing	0.3	−1.6	0.1	−1.6
Services	1.0	1.4	2.1	3.3

1. The service sector includes trade and transport, banking, insurance and miscellaneous services.
2. Value added at constant 1991 prices divided by employment (including self-employed).
3. Average gross yearly earnings (including employers' social security contributions) per employee (excluding self-employed).
4. Nominal wage (as defined in note 3) divided by the product of the value added deflator and labour productivity (as defined in note 2). Equivalent to labour's share of value added.
Source: Sachverständigenrat zur Begutachtung der gesamtwirtschaftlichen Entwicklung, *Jahresgutachten 1993/1994.*

shift partly has reflected the highly European-oriented structure of German exports, where market growth was considerably below world market growth during the recent recession, as well as the need to redirect German production from exports to eastern Germany. But it may also be traced to developments in competitiveness,[33] as measured by the net outcome of changes in relative unit labour costs in manufacturing and changes in the exchange rate.

Non-price factors are also important in Germany's case, where quality, reputation, after-sales service, market structure and marketing strategy have been critical to export success. With high product differentiation, temporary monopoly positions arise on world markets and are renewed with each improvement in product quality, allowing relative export prices/wages to rise, imparting terms of trade gains. Thus, a persistently rising real exchange rate should denote competi-

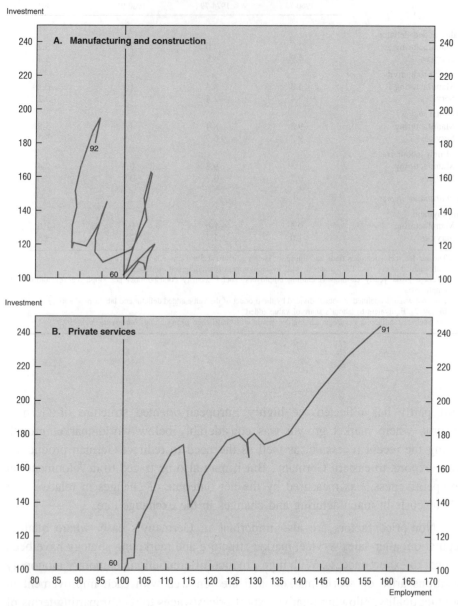

Diagram 24. **INVESTMENT AND EMPLOYMENT
IN MANUFACTURING AND SERVICES**

West Germany, 1960-92, volume indices, 1960 = 100

Investment

A. Manufacturing and construction

Investment

B. Private services

Employment

Source: OECD, *National Accounts*; Sachverständigenrat.

80

Table 24.   **World market shares of three major competitors**

Share of:	1973			1992		
	Germany	Japan-NIEs	United States	Germany[1]	Japan-NIEs	United States
Share in:						
North-South American market[2]	6.7	14.5	19.3	5.1	25.4	21.5
East Asia market[3]	3.9	20.7	19.8	2.5	22.7	12.5
European market[4]	16.6	3.5	7.6	18.0	6.8	6.6
World	12.9	10.1	13.6	11.9	17.9	12.3

1.   Unified Germany.
2.   United States, Canada, Caribbean Islands and Latin America.
3.   Japan, dynamic Asian economies, China, India, Indonesia.
4.   Western and Eastern Europe.
Source: OECD, *Statistics of Foreign Trade*; IMF, Direction of Trade Statistics, *Yearbook.*

tive strength rather than too high costs. Prior to unification, German competitiveness was on such an improving trend, as growing export market shares co-existed with a secular DM-appreciation (Diagram 3 above). Wage growth since the mid-1970s was kept low, and this was reflected in a wage share that declined faster than in most competitor countries (Table 25).

By contrast, the large appreciation of the exchange rate which followed unification was associated with a loss of wage discipline. The double wage and exchange rate shocks resulted in a rise in the real exchange rate of 15 per cent over the 1990-92 period that clearly was not matched by higher non-price competitiveness. Hence a large loss in German competitiveness ensued and export performance worsened considerably.[34] More recently, these post-unification competitiveness losses have been contained, as industrial productivity has been boosted through massive labour shedding and the 1994 wage agreements have resulted in real wage falls. This is consistent with the normal historical pattern of real wage and employment flexibility with regard to external competitiveness. However, Germany's trading partners have also acted to improve their international competitiveness by reducing wages and work forces. Overall, therefore, Germany's international cost competitiveness seems to have improved only modestly.

Alternative measures of the international cost competitiveness of the German economy, on the other hand, suggest that Germany's competitive posi-

Table 25. **Labour share and the tax wedge**

Average over period:	Labour's share [1]			Tax wedge [2]		
	Germany [3]	United States	EC	Germany [3]	United States	EC
1961-64	63.9	69.7	63.1	139.4	123.1	..
1965-69	65.6	70.6	63.3	142.9	125.9	..
1970-73	69.9	74.2	66.1	155.0	128.8	..
1974-79	73.5	74.2	70.1	168.5	131.8	157.1
1980-84	75.5	75.4	71.0	168.3	135.5	165.5
1985-90	71.5	74.6	67.3	172.7	136.6	173.7
1991-93	71.2	75.4 [4]	67.7 [4]	174.0	133.9	177.2 [4]

1. Total wage bill divided by national income at factor cost.
2. Gross compensation of employees divided by net take-home pay.
3. Western Germany.
4. 1991-92.
Source: W. Franz and R.J. Gordon, "German and American wage and price dynamics", European Economic Review, 37 (1993); OECD.

tion may have been holding up much better than suggested by relative manufacturing unit labour costs. This might be concluded from the development of relative manufacturing export prices (Diagram 3, panel B), which in fact shows no decline in price competitiveness since unification, although a sharp squeeze on manufacturing sector profits – which ultimately could undermine competitiveness via the contraction of investment – may also be indicated. Yet broader definitions of the real exchange rate, such as relative unit labour costs in the business sector or relative deflators of total expenditure, also show a more favourable development, especially during the 1980s when unit labour cost growth in the services sector was relatively low.

Lagging technological competitiveness?

Relative productivity levels in manufacturing could, in part, reflect levels of technological competitiveness. Diagram 25 (panel A) shows that Germany's manufacturing productivity disadvantage vis-à-vis the United States, which was the smallest of any country up until 1979, has since been widening. (For the economy as a whole, the productivity gap against the United States continued to narrow, due to the continuing "catch-up" in non-manufacturing output, allowing relative per capita incomes to be maintained [Diagram 25, panel B].) Thus, even though overall cost competitiveness did not start to decline until after 1990,

Diagram 25. **PRODUCTIVITY IN MANUFACTURING
AND GDP PER CAPITA**

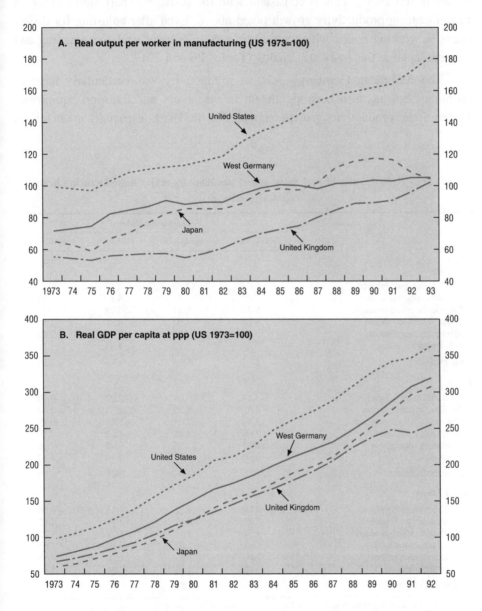

A. Real output per worker in manufacturing (US 1973=100)

United States

West Germany

Japan

United Kingdom

B. Real GDP per capita at ppp (US 1973=100)

West Germany

United States

United Kingdom

Japan

Source: Baily M., G. Burtless and R. E. Litan, *Growth with Equity: Economic Policymaking for the Next Century,*
The Brookings Institution, Washington, D.C., 1993; OECD.

83

underlying technological competitiveness had probably already started falling earlier in the 1980s. This is consistent with the relatively sharp deceleration in manufacturing productivity growth noted above. Even after adjusting for differences in working hours, which would improve Germany's relative standing and worsen Japan's, this story still stands (Tables 26 and 27).[35]

The decline in Germany's relative productivity was particularly large in chemicals but has also been significant in machinery and transport equipment. United States productivity growth recovered in the 1980s, especially in chemicals

Table 26. **Growth rates of real value added per hour by major manufacturing branch**
Annual averages

	Real value added/hour			
	1950-1965 [1]	1965-1973	1973-1979	1979-1990
Germany				
Food, beverages, tobacco	5.74	2.80	3.51	0.79
Textiles, apparel, leather	7.29	3.24	4.80	2.89
Chemicals, allied products	8.20	8.03	3.98	0.33
Basic, fabricated metals	5.24	4.60	4.38	1.89
Machinery, equipment	6.42	4.52	4.67	2.25
Other manufacturing	6.29	5.22	3.54	1.36
Total manufacturing	6.53	5.11	4.44	1.80
Japan				
Food, beverages, tobacco	3.11	10.06	2.23	−0.07
Textiles, apparel, leather	8.05	7.36	4.34	1.42
Chemicals, allied products	13.88	12.04	5.69	3.99
Basic, fabricated metals	7.95	14.85	4.82	2.20
Machinery, equipment	14.10	12.80	9.07	7.96
Other manufacturing	10.50	9.72	3.66	4.47
Total manufacturing	7.75	11.04	5.42	4.88
United States				
Food, beverages, tobacco	3.17	4.32	2.13	0.58
Textiles, apparel, leather	3.27	2.77	3.78	2.65
Chemicals, allied products	3.37	3.51	1.28	3.32
Basic, fabricated metals	1.45	1.67	−0.59	1.05
Machinery, equipment	2.46	2.52	1.12	4.47
Other manufacturing	2.77	2.68	0.96	1.46
Total manufacturing	2.76	2.81	1.27	2.82

1. 1955-65 for Japan; the 1950-65 growth rate for total manufacturing is 8.5 per cent.
Source: Bart van Ark and Dirk Pilat, "Productivity Levels in Germany, Japan and the United States: Differences and Causes", Brookings Papers, *Microeconomics 2*, 1993.

Table 27. **Comparison of value added per hour worked in major manufacturing branches, 1950-90**

Branch	1950[1]	1965	1973	1979	1990
	United States = 100				
Germany/United States					
Food, beverages, tobacco	53.1	76.9	68.4	74.1	75.8
Textiles, apparel, leather	44.0	78.1	81.0	85.9	88.2
Chemicals, allied products	32.4	64.3	90.5	106.0	76.7
Basic, fabricated metals	30.9	53.6	67.2	90.1	98.8
Machinery, equipment	43.7	77.1	90.0	110.7	87.6
Other manufacturing	34.2	56.6	68.8	80.1	79.3
Total manufacturing	38.9	66.7	79.7	95.8	85.9
	Japan = 100				
Germany/Japan					
Food, beverages, tobacco	198.9	298.1	173.2	186.2	204.9
Textiles, apparel, leather	178.1	208.3	152.3	156.5	183.8
Chemicals, allied products	249.2	200.3	149.8	135.9	91.5
Basic, fabricated metals	247.2	232.0	109.4	106.9	103.3
Machinery, equipment	546.3	328.1	177.9	139.1	76.6
Other manufacturing	352.6	283.0	202.4	201.3	144.4
Total manufacturing	234.3	250.8	162.0	153.0	110.3

1. 1955 for Japan.
Source: Van Ark and Pilat, *op. cit.*

and machinery and transport equipment, posting much faster rates than Germany and exacerbating the diverging trend in productivity performance. As a result, Germany lost much of the ground that it had made up prior to the 1980s. Indeed, this deterioration occurred in sectors where Germany had been the clear world leader in 1979. At the same time, Japan has taken a substantial productivity lead over Germany in machinery and equipment, though it lags in overall manufacturing due to a poor performance in food and textiles manufacture.

A variety of factors could in principle account for the divergence in productivity trends. Capital intensity, labour force characteristics (vocational qualifications, age, gender structure), industrial structure (composition of the manufacturing sector) and plant size can, however, be excluded as major explanatory factors. Differences in capital intensity explain only a negligible part of the difference in productivity levels between Germany and the United States at the end of the 1980s, virtually all of the difference in labour productivity being accounted for by total factor productivity (Annex III). Educational attainment levels were similar to those in the United States and Japan after accounting for Germany's vocational training schemes; and Germany's industrial structure was not (despite subsidies) an adverse factor, because of the high concentration of German manufacturing in branches with relatively high absolute productivity levels.[36] Moreover, German industry (contrary to that of Japan) has been characterised by relatively large plants in the two areas where data suggest the greatest weakening in relative productivity performance – chemicals and machinery and transport – ruling out a failure to exploit economies of scale (Table 28).[37]

This leaves technological progress as the possible prime factor behind the manufacturing productivity lag.[38] In particular, this may be a question of innovative dynamism and R&D potency. Here, however, the data is open to interpretation. On the one hand, Germany's strong trade performance and reputation for product quality seem to provide indirect evidence of innovative success and continuing technological leadership. Also, the average age of the capital stock is currently low in international terms, which by itself should make for a relatively high level of technological embodiment. R&D expenditures by business and government, as a ratio to GDP, are no lower than the average of other countries (Table 29). There is a strong revealed comparative advantage in many products

Table 28. **Plant size by manufacturing branch**

Average median size of manufacturing units by number of employees[1]

Branch	Germany	Japan	United States
Food, beverages, tobacco	31	52	274
Textiles, apparel, leather	112	26	233
Chemicals, allied products	723	107	240
Basic, fabricated metals	248	48	208
Machinery, equipment	889	195	633
Other manufacturing	79	28	198
Total manufacturing			
Median size	318	166	263
Average size	30	16	49

1. In 1987.
Source: Van Ark and Pilat, *op. cit.*

86

Table 29. **R&D input by government and business** [1]

1991; per cent of GDP

| | Government [2] | Business sector | | Total | of which: government (direct and indirect) |
		Total	of which: financed by government		
Germany [3]	0.81	1.76	0.19	2.58	1.00
United States [3]	0.77	1.88	0.53	2.74	1.30
Japan	0.77	2.16	0.03	3.05	0.80
France [3]	0.90	1.44	0.32	2.36	1.22
United Kingdom	0.64	1.36	0.20	2.08	0.84
Netherlands	0.85	1.02	0.08	1.91	0.93
Sweden	0.93	1.97	0.23	2.90	1.16
Norway	0.84	1.00	0.16	1.84	1.00
Denmark	0.68	0.99	0.08	1.69	0.76

1. By performance sector.
2. Including higher education institutions.
3. 1992.
Source: OECD, *Main Science and Technology Indicators.*

that, according to OECD classifications, are medium-technology but could equally be considered as "advanced" technology (*e.g.* machine tools) (Diagram 26, upper right-hand quadrant). Germany's revealed comparative advantage in such fields surpasses, in the aggregate, that of all other countries (Table 30). Moreover, there is a comparative advantage in traditional high-technology areas such as electrical machinery and scientific instruments.

On the other hand, another array of indicators – ones that could be considered to be less static and more forward-looking – tend to support the thesis of an innovation lag. First, the comparative advantage in several traditional export industries (*e.g.* chemicals, machinery, and cars), has been declining in recent years (Diagram 26, upper left-hand quadrant). In the majority of products that are classified by the OECD as high-technology (*e.g.* office machines and computers, telecommunications equipment, aircraft, audio-visual equipment, information technology), Germany displays a comparative disadvantage (Diagram 26, lower quadrants). In such areas Germany has fallen behind not only the United States and Japan, but also such European countries as Switzerland, the United Kingdom, and France. Further, the number of new patent registrations, a proxy for innovation output, shows that between 1970 and 1990, innovations in the United

Diagram 26. **REVEALED COMPARATIVE ADVANTAGE IN MANUFACTURING**[1]
West Germany

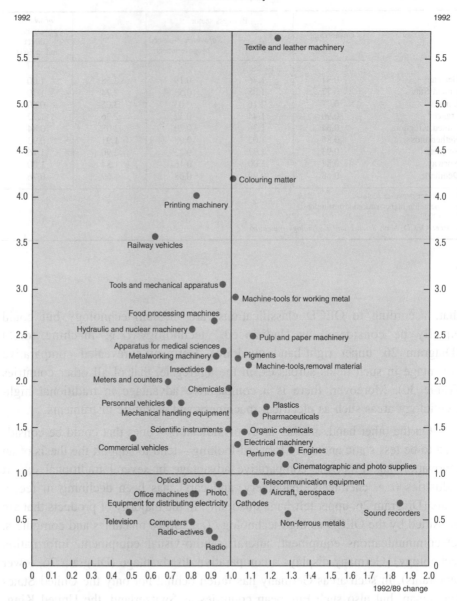

1. Ratio of exports to imports for a given product divided by ratio of exports to imports for manufacturing,
   at current prices.
Source: Sachverständigenrat.

Table 30.   **Comparative advantage in high, medium and low-tech trade**

	Japan		United States		EU		Germany	
	1970	1992	1970	1992	1970	1992	1970	1992
High tech	1.24	1.44	1.59	1.51	0.86	0.82	0.97	0.82
Medium tech	0.78	1.14	1.10	0.90	1.03	1.01	1.25	1.19
Low tech	1.13	0.46	0.67	0.64	1.03	1.13	0.76	0.85

Note: The specialisation (or revealed comparative advantage) index for a particular type of industry has been calculated by dividing the share of a country's exports in a particular industry relative to its total manufacturing exports by the total OECD exports in that industry type relative to the total OECD manufacturing exports. See OECD, *Industrial policy in OECD countries, Annual Review,* 1993, p. 84, for industry classifications.
Source: OECD STAN database; EAS Division.

States and Japan increased substantially, while Germany's share declined in the 1980s, and at an accelerating pace (Diagram 27, panel A). By sector, Germany had a strong showing in motor vehicles and machines, but a weaker showing in chemicals and electronics, while its position is extremely weak in computers and in biotechnology products (panels B and C).[39] While such measures of innovativeness are imprecise and largely suggestive,[40] they seem to be consistent with the observed slippage in manufacturing total factor productivity.

A further, albeit not unambiguous, indicator of competitiveness is given by net direct investment flows. Both outflows and inflows may reflect such factors as European integration and export complementarity. Nevertheless, Germany's direct investment outflows in relation to total OECD outflows (scaled for the relative size of the economies) far exceed inflows as a proportion of total OECD inflows (Diagram 28), suggesting that even allowing for such internationalisation effects, there may remain a net disincentive for capital to remain in (western) Germany.

Assessment of underlying trends

The above review of growth, employment, productivity and competitiveness trends leads to the following main conclusions:

–   Though cost competitiveness has deteriorated in the last few years, Germany remains strong in traditional exports of quality engineering products, mainly to the internal European market where Germany still

Diagram 27. **INDICATORS OF INNOVATION**

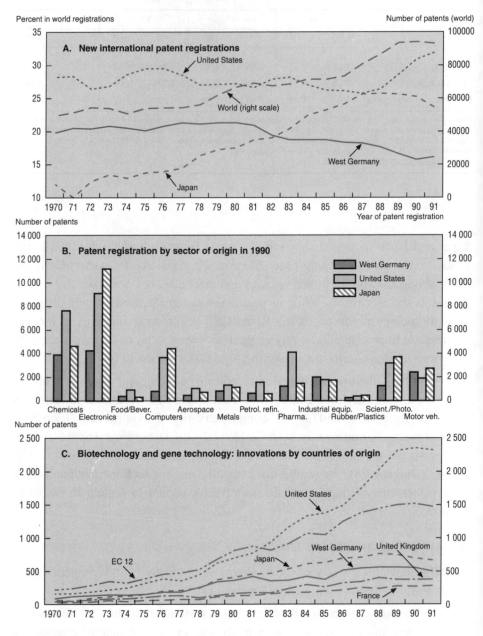

Percent in world registrations

Number of patents (world)

A. New international patent registrations

United States

World (right scale)

West Germany

Japan

Year of patent registration

Number of patents

B. Patent registration by sector of origin in 1990

West Germany
United States
Japan

Chemicals Food/Bever. Aerospace Petrol. refin. Industrial equip. Scient./Photo.
Electronics Computers Metals Pharma. Rubber/Plastics Motor veh.

Number of patents

C. Biotechnology and gene technology: innovations by countries of origin

United States

West Germany United Kingdom

EC 12 Japan

France

Source: EPIDOS/INPADOC, Ifo Patentstatistik.

Diagram 28. **DIRECT INVESTMENT FLOWS**[1]
Ratio OECD=1

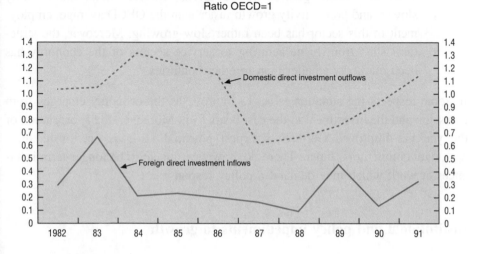

1. German investment as per cent of German value added relative to OECD investment as per cent of OECD value added; unified Germany as of 1991.
Source: OECD, *International Direct Investment.*

clearly dominates. Cost competitiveness, moreover, is slowly being re-established through traditionally high aggregate wage and employment flexibility evident during the recent recession.

– At the same time, German productivity growth has been decelerating faster than the OECD average and it is no longer the world leader in the sectors – chemicals and machinery and transport equipment – that it formerly dominated. Though the deterioration is by no means dramatic, and productivity on a per-hour basis is still the highest in Europe, the trend *vis-à-vis* the major non-European competitors is a matter of concern. The main problem seems to be that German innovation is relatively undynamic, particularly in state-of-the-art sectors, and this has been reflected in a relatively marked slowdown in total factor productivity growth in manufacturing. This has also been reflected in a loss of product market shares to Japan and some other Asian competitors in markets outside Europe.

–   With investment growth in the private service sector significantly slower, and productivity growth faster than the OECD average, employment in this sector has been rather slow-growing. Moreover, the structural shift from manufacturing to service sectors of the economy has been markedly smaller than in other countries.

In some respects the situation is set to improve as the economy emerges from recession and the investment in the east bears fruit. Moreover, the appreciation of the yen has improved Germany's export potential *vis-à-vis* one of its most important competitors, Japan. There do, however, appear to be longer-term influences at work which may demand a policy response.

Institutional and policy impediments to growth

The institutional factors behind the above trends are complex. They relate, on the one hand, to cost factors which could be corrected by several years of wage moderation, but which may also be more permanent insofar as they derive from increases in non-wage costs and inter-sectoral profitability differentials which are still too low due to marked inter-sectoral wage rigidity. They may also derive from skill mismatches arising from insufficient flexibility in training or disincentive effects of unemployment schemes combined with a lack of innovative dynamism. Perhaps most importantly, they stem from the impact of regulations and other barriers to entry, which hamper the development of certain important sectors.[41]

The sources of high costs

Labour market institutions and regulations

Converting by the actual dollar/DM exchange rates, labour costs appear 50 per cent higher than in the United States (Table 31). In aggregate, wages are generally sensitive to macroeconomic conditions while wage contracts display a certain degree of uniformity.[42] The Council of Economic Advisors defines a norm for allowable wage increases as the sum of expected productivity growth per hour plus "unavoidable" inflation, with moderation called for in periods of high unemployment but with no allowance for tax increases (except employers' con-

Table 31. **International comparison of labour costs**
In manufacturing

	Western Germany		United States			Japan		
	DM	Percentage change from 1985	DM equivalent	Percentage change from 1985	Index Germany = 100	DM equivalent	Percentage change from 1985	Index Germany = 100
Effective wage per man hour								
1985	21.96		30.76		140	16.19		74
1990	27.01	23.0	19.96	−35.1	74	17.36	7.2	64
1993 June[1]	30.40	38.4	20.33	−33.9	67	27.53	70.0	91
Average wages per worker								
1985	36 416		59 211		163	35 098		96
1990	43 159	18.5	36 717	−38.0	85	36 874	5.1	85
1993 June[1]	47 783	31.2	40 299	−31.9	84	54 127	54.2	113
Exchange rates			DM/dollar			DM/yen		
1985			2.926			0.0123		
1990			1.613	−44.9		0.0112	−9.3	
1993 June[1]			1.652	−43.5		0.0154	25.0	

1. 1993 June data are calculated using the wage data in 1992 converted by the exchange rate in June 1993.
Source: Ministry of Labour of Japan, *Monthly Labour Survey*; EC Department of Statistics, *Labour Costs*; OECD.

tributions to social security contributions which are seen as reducing the room for wage increases). The unions have followed this model by and large, though usually demanding compensation for tax increases and for expected *total* inflation.

Though industry-wide wage contracting may provide macroeconomic wage flexibility, there has been little wage adjustment to changing labour market conditions in particular sectors, skills, and regions. Contrary to other industrial countries, the dispersion of earnings in Germany decreased slightly during the 1980s, as employees at the bottom of the income distribution narrowed the gap with median wage earners, in some part due to "social components" in wage agreements.[43] Evidence from the industrial sector alone is more ambiguous, however, as between 1970 and 1992 average hourly earnings increased at (nearly) the same rate for workers of all categories. Nevertheless, viewed against the background that the ratio of unskilled and low qualified workers shrank substantially, with unemployment among these groups being especially high, greater wage flexibility might have been expected. The wage bargaining process, however, has been more strongly influenced by the desire to reinforce the position of low-paid insiders than by the desire to let unemployed outsiders bid themselves into a job.[44] As sectoral wage ratios are also rather sticky, job creation in the service sector was too weak to absorb the low qualified unemployed in the context of a growing labour force. The regional wage structure also points to labour market rigidities. The relative differences in hourly earnings between western German Länder decreased over the past fifteen years, despite growing differences in regional unemployment rates.[45] With mobility in Germany being relatively low, regional labour market problems – which are to a large extent sectoral problems caused by structural change – are not rapidly mitigated by migration.

Over the past ten years "official" weekly working hours, as laid down in collective agreements, were reduced by about 5 per cent on average, *i.e.* roughly two hours for a full-time employee. With respect to unit labour costs this would not necessarily have been a disadvantage for German producers if the reduction was either compensated by a higher productivity growth or by appropriate wage restraint. There are, indeed, indications that hourly productivity increased faster – about ¾ per cent per year economy-wide – than per capita productivity, thus implying a marginal compensation for firms. But the reduction of working hours was only partially incorporated into the wage formula, leading to permanent cost increases. Additional damaging effects have also arisen from the fact that the supply of qualified labour has been "artificially" reduced: average yearly working hours in Germany are up to one-third less than in competitor countries. This shortage was particularly strongly felt during the unification boom. Furthermore, Germany has not been very successful in "decoupling" equipment run-times (Maschinenlaufzeiten) from individual working hours. Enterprises in Belgium, the Netherlands, or the United Kingdom can use their machines significantly longer than German firms. Therefore, a reduction of the working week goes hand in hand with a low degree of capital utilisation.

Job security is regulated through a complex legal framework of protection against dismissal, although in 1985 the government partially liberalised this with the Employment Promotion Act, which extended the permitted period for fixed-term contracts from six to eighteen months.[46] For workers with permanent contracts, lay-offs are possible but expensive: above a certain minimum, the firm must present a "social plan" which includes substantial funding for social support and retraining. Dismissals are often challenged through the courts, who may by-pass economic efficiency criteria in favour of social equalisation goals. Moreover, there is a fundamental contradiction in that job-security regulations, by making lay-offs more expensive, discourage hiring by firms and hence deny job security to labour market outsiders. Active labour market policies are thus an important tool for fighting long-term unemployment. Wage subsidies are given for the hiring of workers over 50 and for the re-integration of the long-term unemployed. However, they are short term in nature (one to three years) and have not been very effective, especially in light of the inflow of skilled labour from eastern Europe. While spending for vocational training has doubled over the last ten years, it has largely neglected the *re*-training of the long-term unemployed, which constitutes the core of the problem. Qualification certification requirements for most job descriptions further exacerbate the insider/outsider problem in labour markets.[47]

Taxes and social charges

In the wake of German reunification, the supply-side strategy of progressive income tax relief implemented since 1986 gave way to comprehensive tax increases. As a result, the overall tax burden, including social security charges, after having bottomed out in 1990 at 40.2 per cent of GDP, rose to a record level of 43.6 per cent in 1993. Of the major industrialised countries, only France has a higher share, while in Japan and the United States the burden is around 30 per cent (Table 32). This increase was mainly due to higher indirect taxes – in particular a rise in the VAT from 14 to 15 per cent – and higher social contributions to the Labour Office, the pension insurance scheme and the health care system (Diagram 29). The overall tax burden is expected to rise further to more than 45 per cent in 1995, with a net increase in the long-term insurance contribution rate, the reimposition of the solidarity income tax surcharge and introduction of a new long-term care insurance scheme. At that time the social charges on the liable gross working wage will rise to nearly 40 per cent, compared with 35 per cent in the late 1980s.

Although a policy of increasing taxes was justified so as to limit the deterioration in the public deficit, it is clearly suboptimal. Apart from their long-term

Table 32. **Effective tax rates**

Various countries, in percentage

	Overall effective tax rate [1]		Income tax rate [2]		Employers' tax rate [3]		Indirect tax rate less subsidies [4]	
	1973	1993	1973	1993	1973	1993	1973	1993
Germany	**40.2**	**43.6**	**22.3**	**23.6**	**15.9**	**19.1**	**11.2**	**11.7**
Austria	40.6	46.6	22.8	26.7	13.9	18.2	16.2	13.1
Belgium	38.0	46.5	25.1	29.8	14.4	25.6	8.6	9.8
Denmark	43.1	50.3	45.9	55.8	0.7	0.9	13.7	13.7
Finland	35.1	47.2	27.1	27.3	19.2	26.7	10.9	11.8
France	36.0	44.5	13.7	17.4	23.6	28.1	12.9	12.2
Italy	26.3	43.3	11.3	36.4	27.8	29.6	6.8	9.7
Japan	21.1	30.5	19.3	22.5	8.2	14.9	6.0	7.1
Netherlands	42.3	48.8	25.9	31.6	18.5	10.9	9.6	10.0
Norway	47.4	45.9	27.9	33.2	14.9	13.5	12.8	10.8
Sweden	42.4	50.6	31.5	35.5	14.8	26.2	12.6	9.5
United Kingdom	31.3	32.2	21.1	20.7	10.2	12.5	11.5	13.3
United States	30.3	30.9	23.4	22.7	12.8	18.3	8.8	8.2
Average [5]	36.5	43.1	24.4	29.5	15.0	18.8	10.9	10.8

1. Taxes and social security contributions as a percentage of GDP.
2. Expressed as a percentage of individual's compensation.
3. Pension and social security contributions as a percentage of wages and salaries (aggregate economy).
4. Expressed as a percentage of nominal GDP in factor prices.
5. Unweighted.
Source: OECD.

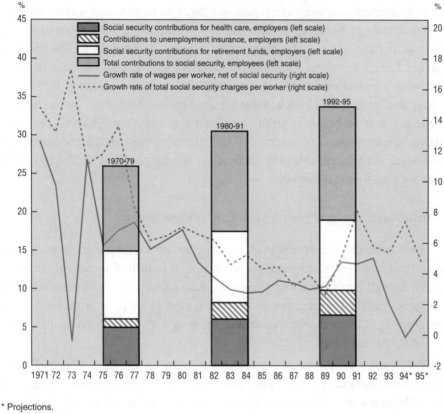

Diagram 29. **SOCIAL SECURITY CHARGES**

West Germany, in per cent of total labour costs

Social security contributions for health care, employers (left scale)
Contributions to unemployment insurance, employers (left scale)
Social security contributions for retirement funds, employers (left scale)
Total contributions to social security, employees (left scale)
Growth rate of wages per worker, net of social security (right scale)
Growth rate of total social security charges per worker (right scale)

1970-79   1980-91   1992-95

1971 72 73 74 75 76 77 78 79 80 81 82 83 84 85 86 87 88 89 90 91 92 93 94* 95*

* Projections.
Source: OECD.

negative supply effects, tax increases have apparently affected the level of negotiated pay rates and thus, in addition to the direct impact of indirect taxes on prices,
had unfavourable repercussions on prices and ultimately also on corporate capital
formation.

As a result of the tax-reduction policies pursued by other countries, the
German corporate tax system stands out for its extensive array of exemptions but
relatively high rates (50 per cent for retained profits compared with 35 per cent in
the United States, $37\frac{1}{2}$ per cent in Japan and $33\frac{1}{3}$ per cent in France). Likewise,

the statutory top marginal tax rate on personal income, at 53 per cent, remains high by international standards. As indirect taxes are less likely to discourage saving, investment and work effort than are taxes on income and wealth, emphasis is switching to reducing income tax rates. An easing of the corporate tax burden in particular is on the government's agenda, mainly with the view to attracting foreign investors and retaining German ones. A start has been made in 1994, with a reduction in the tax rate from 36 to 30 per cent for distributed earnings and from 50 to 45 per cent for retained profits. Moreover, for the income tax, the top rate on business profits has been reduced from 53 to 47 per cent. However, the corporate tax burden will on balance remain unchanged, given the above-noted 7$\frac{1}{2}$ per cent solidarity income tax surcharge which applies to corporate as well as personal tax bills.

Insufficient competitive pressure in service sectors

The degree of competition in the service sector has important implications both for employment creation and for the prices of industrial inputs, which are a factor in overall economy competitiveness. Accordingly, the government has in recent years pursued a programme of deregulation of services, a process given momentum by European integration and the single market. Progress has been substantial, but uneven.

With respect to *rail transport*, at the beginning of 1994 the "Bahnreform" (reform of the railways) became effective, motivated by the fact that the national railways have not only lost ground in the transportation market – its market share shrank from roughly 25 per cent in 1980 to 16 per cent in 1990 – but also proved to be a growing burden for public budgets: Federal government expenditures for the railways are estimated to have reached DM 32 billion in 1994 (including higher costs due to the fusion of the east and west German railway companies). Under a publicly-owned joint stock company, four separate units (short-distance and long distance passenger traffic, freight traffic and the rail network) have been established. Since January 1994, the Federal Government has been responsible for investment in the rail network, the corresponding "railway unit" being charged with the depreciation. Pricing the lines according to demand and maintenance costs could stop cross-subsidisation of services and transmit clearer price signals to local authorities and consumers. More generally, in a medium-term perspective, the new organisational structure – despite not being a "real" privatisation – should lead to a more efficient management of the railways and to better cost transparency, thereby stimulating competition in the transportation sector.

The reform package includes the establishment of a new subsidiary budget, the Federal Railways Fund (Bundeseisenbahnvermögen), which has assumed the debts incurred by the railways (approximately DM 66 billion). The staff of the railways, for legal reasons now employed by the Federal Railways Fund and "loaned out" to the operational units, is expected to be reduced by more than 100 000 persons by the end of the decade.[48] It is envisaged that the responsibility for short-distance passenger traffic will be transferred to the Länder in 1996, which, in exchange, will be compensated for this loss-making operation by the Federal Government. If a competitive bidding were to be established, the most efficient railway company – public or private, domestic or foreign – could then be chosen to supply the transport services.

As far as the *telecommunications industry* is concerned, the so-called "Postreform I", entering into effect in mid-1989, divided the federal post office (Deutsche Bundespost) into three public enterprises (postal service, post-bank and telecommunications) and opened parts of the telecommunications market to competition: the market for equipment has been liberalised, some private services (teletext, satellite communications, mobile functions) have been allowed – newcomers using either existing infrastructure, or establishing new networks. With Telekom's monopoly on terrestrial telecommunications networks remaining untouched and its legal status as a public enterprise restricting international activities as well as ambitious investment programmes, charges remain high (Diagram 30), and further reform has been regarded as inevitable (see below).

The main impetus to deregulate the highly fragmented and monopolised German *energy markets* stems from the European Commission. Original plans aimed at a liberalisation as part of the Single Market, but it soon turned out to be extremely difficult to break open national or regional (electricity or gas supply) monopolies or to stop subsidisation (of coal, for example). Discussion focuses now, *inter alia*, on private investment in networks that "are often hampered by administrative constraints" and on third-party access to networks.[49] While some countries have made progress in deregulating energy distribution and in privatisation of utilities, Germany (among other countries) seems to be lagging behind. With respect to competitiveness of German electricity-consuming enterprises this

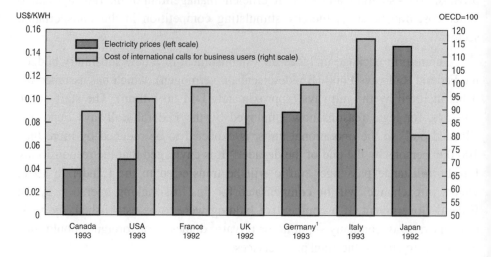

Diagram 30. **ELECTRICITY PRICES AND TELEPHONE CHARGES**

US$/KWH   OECD=100

Legend:
- Electricity prices (left scale)
- Cost of international calls for business users (right scale)

Countries: Canada 1993, USA 1993, France 1992, UK 1992, Germany[1] 1993, Italy 1993, Japan 1992

Cross country comparison is impaired by the fluctuations of the exchange rates.
1. West Germany.
Source: IEA Statistics 4/1993; OECD, *Communications Outlook 1993.*

is a clear disadvantage, as electricity prices are considerably higher than for most of their foreign counterparts.

As far as *distribution* is concerned, Germany is one of the most regulated markets in the OECD, especially with respect to shop opening hours. Nevertheless, in retail trade, competition seems to be still vigorous, despite growing concentration in some markets. The overall number of enterprises increased by 9 per cent between 1980 and 1990, the highest growth rates occurring in trade in electronics and electrical products, cars, motor-cycles, and bicycles. On the other hand, in grocery retailing many shop-owners terminated business or lost their independence; the market share of the ten largest trading firms in this sector is on an upward trend and amounted to 60 per cent in 1992. Apparently, this does not hamper innovation and imitation in retail trade, as advanced organisational structures, new distribution channels or the development of markets abroad are introduced by all types of trading firms and – if successful – rapidly copied.[50]

In the remaining service sectors, the regulatory situation may be summarised as follows.[51] In *banking*, major liberalisation and deregulation steps were already taken in the 1960s and there has been some additional deregulation activity in recent years, for example, the amendment of the German banking law in conformity with the Basle Capital Accords and various EC banking directives. Existing regulations are thus relatively light (as in the United Kingdom and the Netherlands) and competition relatively high. In *insurance*, the regulatory system is, in effect, relatively restrictive, with a comparatively low share of foreign interests, due to the entrenched positions held by large local insurance companies. However, ongoing mandatory implementation of recent EC insurance directives should ensure greater competition in the market. Regarding *road transport*, regulation has imposed particularly strong barriers to entry in Germany and the degree of internationalisation of national transporters is relatively low. In *air transport*, each EC member state has been traditionally dominated by a single flag carrier. Germany's carrier is being scheduled for privatisation in 1994, following a period of restructuring which is seen as giving the national airline a strong competitive advantage. The highly regulated *liberal professions* have recently been given more room for manœuvre by a reform of the regulations governing lawyers and accountants, with limited advertising and the formation of incorporated partnerships (Partnerschaftsgesellschaften) now being permitted.

Subsidies

Subsidies, though clearly trending down, remain a major instrument of protection in the non-service sectors. Counting direct cash grants, tax concessions, and soft loans provided at all levels of government,[52] plus agricultural subsidies channelled through the EC fund, subsidies to western German enterprises are estimated to have declined from around 4 per cent of GDP in 1980 to 3 per cent currently, while rising to around 4½ per cent of GDP for Germany as a whole (Table 33). The reduction of western German subsidy levels, which helped to make room for new subsidies to the east, was accomplished almost exclusively through efforts at the federal level: federal subsidies declined from 1.7 to 0.7 per cent of GDP between 1980 and 1994, and, under the government's financial plan, are to be cut by another one quarter by 1997 (with no change for Germany as a whole).

Despite progress, subsidies could still be considered too high from the viewpoint of economic efficiency as well as in international terms.[53] While about half of all subsidies to the business sector go for regional structural adjustment

Table 33. **Subsidies to the business sector**

DM billion

	1980	1989	1990	1991	1992	1993	1994 [1]
Federal subsidies to private enterprises [2]	**24.6**	**29.9**	**30.1**	**37.3**	**37.1**	**36.6**	**37.6**
As a per cent of GDP	*1.7*	*1.3*	*1.3*	*1.3*	*1.2*	*1.2*	*1.2*
To eastern Länder	–	–	–	9.0	11.0	12.6	15.2
Direct subsidies	–	–	–	6.7	6.9	7.7	10.6
Federal tax concessions	–	–	–	2.3	4.1	4.9	5.1
To western Länder	24.6	29.9	30.1	28.3	26.1	23.3	21.8
As a per cent of western GDP	*1.7*	*1.3*	*1.3*	*1.1*	*0.9*	*0.8*	*0.7*
Direct subsidies	12.5	14.1	14.2	13.0	14.1	11.7	10.9
Federal tax concessions	12.1	15.8	15.9	15.3	12.0	11.6	10.9
Subsidies broadly defined [3]	**61.0**	**83.0**	**92.4**	**118.1**	**135.7**	–	–
As a per cent of GDP	*4.1*	*3.7*	*3.9*	*4.2*	*4.4*	–	–
To eastern Länder	–	–	11.5	29.7	49.2	–	–
Grants	–	–	10.7	18.7	20.0	–	–
Tax concessions [4]	–	–	0.8	4.5	7.7	–	–
Soft loans	–	–	–	–	7.6	–	–
Subsidies by the Treuhandanstalt	–	–	–	6.5	14.0	–	–
To western Länder	61.0	83.0	80.9	88.4	86.5	–	–
As a per cent of western GDP	*4.1*	*3.7*	*3.9*	*3.3*	*3.1*	–	–
Grants	27.6	40.1	39.5	45.1	48.8	–	–
Tax concessions [4]	30.6	38.8	36.7	37.3	33.0	–	–
Soft loans	2.8	4.1	4.7	6.0	4.7	–	–

1. Preliminary.
2. As measured in the Biannual subsidies report, describing developments in subsidies by the federal government in its about 300 programmes.
3. As measured by the DIW, applying a broader concept than that used by the federal government, as it includes not only federal direct subsidies and tax concessions to private enterprises, but also: *i)* soft loans; *ii)* subsidies of para-government organisations such as the Treuhandanstalt; *iii)* subsidies to public enterprises; *iv)* payments from the EC Fund, in particular in agriculture; *v)* grants to the coalmining industry financed by an earmarked surcharge on electricity charges (the "Kohlepfennig"); *vi)* job-creation facilities financed by unemployment insurance; and *vii)* rent allowances. Due to problems with data collection, grants by the Länder and local authorities are no longer included.
4. Including Länder and local authorities.
Source: Ministry of Finance, *Bericht der Bundesregierung über die Entwicklung der Finanzhilfen des Bundes und der Steuervergünstigungen für die Jahre 1991 bis 1994 (Vierzehnter Subventionsbericht)*, Bonn, August 1993 and preceding issues; and DIW, *Wochenbericht*, No. 46/92, Vol. 59, Berlin 1992.

and housing construction, the tendency for declining industries to be concentrated in poorer regions, as well as the high level of subsidisation at the regional government levels, means that a significant portion of subsidies, in effect, goes to structurally weak sectors such as agriculture, mining, and shipbuilding. Though originally intended to be strictly temporary measures to ease adjustment, intensive lobbying efforts by firms and unions have resulted in most such subsidies becoming quasi-permanent, compensating the sheltered sectors in part for declining external trade barriers. The only "sunrise" industry receiving direct subsidies is aircraft. General subsidies to R&D remain quite low, accounting for only about $1^1/_2$ per cent of total subsidies. Indeed, subsidies to sunset industries take resources away from sunrise industries via higher taxation and interest rates. Thus, the area of subsidies remains an ongoing challenge for policy reform.

Barriers to innovation

Innovations, broadly defined as investments in knowledge,[54] differ from other types of investment because they can be only partially appropriated to the investor by way of patent protection and corporate secrecy practices. Spill-overs of such knowledge, however, benefit society as a whole and are often used as a rationalisation for heavy government involvement in the development of high-tech sectors. However, incentives can easily be distorted by excessive government intervention. Thus, following earlier attempts to promote specific sectors such as electronics, the government has largely backtracked in the face of mixed results. The focus of industrial adjustment policy has been on providing an adequate infrastructure necessary for innovation and technological dissemination (education, standardisation, research infrastructure), with special emphasis on strengthening the innovation capacity of the small and medium-sized enterprises, in addition to general incentives such as tax relief for R&D. In practice, the entire system of training, education, and applied research has been geared primarily to serving those sectors in which Germany has been traditionally strong – in particular through a vast range of specialised technical apprenticeships. This implies an implicit strategy of consolidating gains in areas of revealed comparative advantage. While the private sector has (correctly) been left with the task of identifying which high-technology sectors can be exploited most successfully, human resources have not been moved easily to the new areas (see below).

The financial system

New enterprises are an important vehicle for human capital-intensive (high-technology) investments and their financing is thus a key factor in innovative activity. New ventures are risky (bankruptcy rates can reach 30 to 40 per cent even in the most successfully innovating countries), and tie up capital for a long period of time while the company gets off the ground (perhaps five years). Moreover, rapid changes in technology can wipe out initial monopoly positions very quickly. These risky first years of the new firm's life are often financed in the form of venture capital, where the investors are also responsible for management and continual monitoring of the firm's progress. If the company survives past the break-even point, it can expect sometimes to earn extremely high profit rates, which allows it then to go public or to be absorbed by a larger company (capital gains ratios in the high-tech area can reach 30 or 40 times the value of the initial investment).

The two countries that have been most successful in financing new activities through the market have been Japan and the United States, the former via cheap intermediated capital, the latter via a large and buoyant stock market and an abundant supply of venture capital, which favours the setting up of new firms. By making the threat of market entry by new firms credible, the market-based system favours innovation and forces existing firms to be more competitive; by offering a wide range of opportunities for sale or purchase of firms, it lowers exit barriers which facilitates risk-taking. In Germany, however, as in most of continental Europe, the institution of venture capital is poorly developed. In the German system, commercial banks play an important role in both the allocation of resources to firms and the monitoring of company performance through mostly standing relationships ("house bank" relations). Banks do not just provide their clients with bank credit and payment services, but in addition they supply a broad range of financial and managerial advice, ranging from assistance in raising start-up capital to the sponsoring of equity issues in the stock market. Creditor bank representatives sit directly on (large joint-stock) companies' supervisory boards. The smaller firms, in particular, are dependent on bank finance. These firms are usually owned by private individuals, a group of individuals (Personengesellschaften), or they are run as private limited companies (GmbH) – all having no access to the organised equity markets. Tapping the stock market as an instrument of raising capital is available only to the larger firms that are organised as joint stock companies (Aktiengesellschaften). Despite a surge in issuance activity over the last decade,[55] the absolute number of some 500 listed joint stock companies, and their market capitalisation, is quite small for a country of Germany's size.[56] Due to the importance of small and medium sized companies in Germany, some two-thirds of capital raised externally is provided by banks (Annex III).

Such a system of bank-dominated finance entails both benefits and costs. Academic studies have shown that the close relationship between banks and firms has led to higher productivity and better resource allocation within the firm and in the economy as a whole. Firms with close bank ties have better access to capital and encounter lower costs of capital because of better information sharing between firms and banks.[57] In conventional financial systems, informational asymmetries often lead to sub-optimal credit rationing or onerous lending terms for firms. Bank presence also protects the firm from hostile take-overs, while long-term bank financing encourages firms to take a longer-term view. On the other hand, newer firms without established bank ties may encounter difficulties in securing credit (reportedly a problem in eastern Germany). While there exists a high degree of competition in banking thanks to early liberalisation, the relatively small role played by capital markets in enterprise finance implies a possible lack of market discipline over investment decisions. In particular, there are information and incentive problems in the capital market which are detrimental to innovative investment.

The German government is addressing this problem. The availability of start-up finance is being supported by public credit guarantees and preferential loan conditions which are offered to potential entrepreneurs and investors as part of the general program of support for small and medium-sized companies (Mittelstandsförderung). There are also supporting schemes for the establishment of new firms (Existenzgründung) which are implemented and channelled through the "Kreditanstalt für Wiederaufbau" and other public sector banks: individuals and firms apply for these funds with the assistance of commercial banks which usually co-finance the project of the applying borrower. In addition, in the late 1980s conditions for the provision of venture capital were improved through the Act on "risk capital companies" (Unternehmensbeteiligungsgesellschaften), a kind of "investment company" designed to invest in the venture capital market. Since then, however, only a few firms of this type have been established. The government has taken several steps to improve the conditions for the access of medium sized firms to the stock market by the establishment of a secondary stock exchange market compartment (the so-called Regulated Market, or Geregelter Markt) in 1987 and – more recently – by changes in the Joint Stock Company Act (Aktiengesetz) designed to develop a less formally and rigidly structured organisational form of joint stock company which is more suitable and attractive to smaller companies (Kleine Aktiengesellschaften). And just recently, the regulations on insider trading were adapted towards international standards. Thus, structural deficiencies in the provision of risk capital have diminished. Nevertheless, it is important to make further progress in market-based provision of risk finance.

The regulatory framework in industry

As in the services sector, regulatory policies also tend to inhibit the establishment of new manufacturing firms, especially those proposing new technologies. The main entry barriers are posed by very lengthy licensing procedures (Genehmigungsverfahren), where waits of two years are common while the necessary environmental impact studies, etc., are completed (it reportedly takes as little as six weeks to complete similar procedures in the United States). Basic research, especially in the biotechnology field, tends to be displaced to neighbouring countries such as France, and there is worry about a "brain drain" of the brightest young scientific talents to abroad.[58] Once a new company is established, moreover, it is subject to bureaucratic restrictions such as a reporting burden required by the Gene Technology Law of 1993 (Gentechnikgesetz). Although this law represents a significant step towards deregulation compared with previous practices, companies point out that Germany has not kept pace with progress in deregulation in Japan and the United States in recent years in the biotechnology area. Practices such as these have led to a growing competitive disadvantage for Germany in the human capital-intensive areas. Indeed, patent data for pharmaceuticals and chemicals indicate that virtually all patents are awarded to a small number of large firms – in contrast to the United States, where a large number of patents are given to small and medium-sized firms, reflecting the far easier market entry and access to risk capital and capital markets there.[59]

Human capital

Empirical studies support view that the German youth training system does an impressive job of preparing young people for skilled positions in industrial firms.[60] Under the so-called "dual" apprenticeship system, a young person between the ages of 16 and 25 applies to a prospective employer for an apprenticeship place. If accepted,[61] the trainee enters a two to four year programme during which he receives a low wage (compared to what he would have earned as an unskilled labourer) in exchange for the right to participate in on-the-job training and to follow a designated series of courses in colleges run by the

Länder. By the age of 24, about two-thirds of all young people have obtained an apprenticeship certificate based on performance assessments and on written exams. Training regulations are set by the appropriate union and employer organisations and are ratified by the Ministry of Economics. The Chambers of Commerce enforce the quality regulations for in-firm training. According to survey data, the vast majority of the graduates (about 82 per cent in 1991) reported working in the occupation for which they were trained two to four years after graduation. Since 1980, an increasing proportion of the youth age cohort has sought training places; however, since the size of this cohort has been declining[62] and since the number of places offered by firms has grown, the number of unfilled apprenticeships in the west has tended to increase.

Recently, the potential contribution of these programmes to Germany's future economic prosperity has been questioned. It is thought, in particular, that these programmes offer training in too narrow a range of skills. Apparently as a result of such perceptions, there has been a trend toward greater academic attainment, at both secondary and tertiary levels, among the apprenticeship population. The number of people entering apprenticeships that have passed the rigorous Abitur (university entrance exams) has markedly increased, and more and more youth are opting for university training, either at the outset or upon completion of their apprenticeships. A second charge levelled against the programmes is that they are slow to respond to changes in technology and industrial structure.[63] The slowness of change may reflect the consensual nature of the decision-making process. For example, it took unions and employer representatives much of the 1980s to negotiate a reduction in the number of apprenticeship categories from 465 to 374, in an attempt to eliminate obsolete categories and reduce existing over-specialisation.

This has shifted part of the problem to the university sector – both regular and polytechnic (Fachhochschulen). The university system, which was designed for less than 1 million students, at present has to cope with more than 1.8 million. University enrolments have exploded, as the number of new entrants has grown[64] and as the time taken by students to complete degree requirements has lengthened.[65] The growing budgetary burden, the dissatisfaction with the frictions of the current system, and the central role of education and training in the strategy to improve the competitiveness of the German economy, point to the necessity of a restructuring, and a broad reform discussion is currently taking place.[66] Proposals to enhance the efficiency of the universities focus *inter alia* on four aspects:

- To overcome capacity constraints, the government has called for expansion of higher education institutions, in particular an increase of funds for the Fachhochschulen.
- A bundle of incentives and penalties is needed to shorten the time spent at university.[67] To this end, the intention is also to oblige universities to distinguish between occupation-related basic studies, that could be completed within a fixed period of four or five years, and post-graduate training.
- The autonomy of the universities should be extended with respect to the use of funds and the selection of candidates. To strengthen competition between universities, public funding should be tied to efficiency criteria concerning teaching as well as research.

The underlying purpose of the proposed reforms is to ensure that the university system produces the skills required by a modern, dynamic business sector.

Summing up

The foregoing discussion of institutional conditions lends support to the hypothesis of a highly successful traditional manufacturing export sector coexisting with institutional and regulatory impediments to growth which have inhibited the development of some other sectors. These impediments, which will reduce underlying growth potential even after the economy emerges from the recession, can be traced to the following areas:

- Inter-sectoral wage inflexibility and floors on wages both price low-skilled workers out of the job market and inhibit job-creating investment in the service sectors. At the same time, regulations against dismissals discourage hiring and raise investment risks.
- Entry barriers arising from excessive regulations are prevalent in the modern service sectors and in human capital-intensive manufacturing, exacerbating the problems arising from wage inflexibility.
- Taxes and social charges are high, raising costs for the efficient sectors, while industrial subsidies impede adjustment across a range of traditional industries.

- The provision of risk capital to smaller firms and the supply of venture capital for start-up finance is less market-based than in other countries.
- Training and education systems, though having many positive features, are inadequately geared for change, limiting the economy's innovative potential.

Agenda for reform

In recognition of the above structural problems, the government has been pursuing a programme of supply-side reforms since the mid-1980s, consisting of tax reform, privatisation and deregulation.[68] Services, especially, transport and communication, are being liberalised, either in response to technical progress or within the context of the EC single market programme. The process of liberalisation is thus well advanced (see box). However, the recent Standort Report spelled out plans for a stepped-up pace of reform, and the essential elements of such a programme, as well as suggestions for yet further steps, will now be outlined.

Reforming the welfare state

One of the main tasks of supply-side reform is to bring the tax burden back down to at least pre-unification levels via deeper reductions in public spending. From the supply-side point of view, a prime target for spending control are industrial subsidies, as these directly impede structural change while keeping taxes high. The Council of Economic Advisors has recommended that all existing subsidies and tax expenditures at all levels of government, be phased out, apart from those applying to all firms on a non-discriminatory basis. Any new subsidies, especially those to maintain eastern German "core industries", should be strictly limited in time, perhaps to a maximum of three years, with no exceptions. The problem of labour redundancies should be handled by the normal social safety net and – most important – by faster liberalisation of the labour market and freer entry into service sector markets (below). By contrast, the stance of the

109

Recent measures to improve competitiveness

The following is a record of structural policy measures taken in recent years, with a view to improving incentives and reducing impediments to growth.

Tax reform

- Between 1986 and 1990, a three-tier *income tax reform* package entered into effect. Marginal tax rates were reduced and the tax schedule made more linearly progressive. Net tax reliefs amounted to almost DM 50 billion.
- The 1992 *Tax Amendment Law* included, among other provisions, the first stage of a *corporation tax reform* as of 1993. Improvements to the general tax regulations for enterprises were made by lowering the net worth tax (*Vermögensteuer*) and the trade tax on earnings (*Gewerbeertragsteuer*). Temporary exemption from trading capital tax (*Gewerbekapitalsteuer*) and net worth tax in the new Länder has been extended until end-1994. As part of the whole package, the general VAT rate was raised from 14 to 15 per cent as of 1993.
- In the *Law on Safeguarding Germany's Economic Future (Standortsicherungsgesetz)* corporation and income tax rates have been reduced as of 1994. For the *corporation tax*, the rate on undistributed profits has been lowered from 50 to 45 per cent and on distributed profits from 36 to 30 per cent; for the *income tax*, the top rate on business profits has been reduced from 53 to 47 per cent . Temporary exemption from trading capital tax and net worth tax in the new Länder has been further extended until end-1995. As a – partial – compensation, some tax concessions have been cut and tax loopholes closed. Depreciation allowances on equipment remained untouched.

Non-wage labour costs

- In an attempt to stabilise non-wage labour costs, the *Public Health Structure Law (1992)* stipulated relief measures for the statutory health insurance system. Taking foreseeable demographic tendencies and the distortions of the present system into account, the government has recently announced further reform measures that are intended to reorganise the scale of benefits and to enhance efficiency.
- With respect to the phasing in of an a *long-term care insurance (Pflegeversicherung)* as of 1995, employers, who are liable for 50 per cent of the contributions, will be compensated either by the proposed abolition of a public holiday, or employees will have to pay the full contribution.
- Contributions to pension insurance funds have been increased by 1.7 percentage points as of 1994.

Labour market

- The *Law on Working Time (Arbeitszeitrechtsgesetz)* is designed to improve the flexibility of working time by allowing work on Sundays and public holidays in certain specified cases.

(continued on next page)

(continued)

- According to the *Law on the Promotion of Employment*, fixed-term employment contracts can be concluded more easily; this provision will be maintained until 2000. The same law includes a provision for the establishment of *private employment agencies*. Until now, the Federal Labour Office has had a virtual monopoly on the placement of employees, with exceptions concerning artists and senior management staff.
- As of 1994, most of the *payments of benefits* under unemployment insurance and labour market policy have been reduced by 3 percentage points. For example, unmarried unemployed persons will qualify for unemployment benefits amounting to 60 per cent and unemployment aid equal to 53 per cent of average take-home pay.

Financial markets

- Since the beginning of the 1990s, two laws to promote the development of financial markets have been passed. The first – in addition to measures such as the establishment of a *German Futures and Options Exchange* – removed important disadvantages from German capital markets by abolishing the *exchange turnover tax* as of 1991, and the *company tax* and *tax on drafts and bills of exchange* as of 1992. It also expanded the room for manœuvre for capital investment companies. The second law aims at a better protection of investors by improving market transparency and supervision of securities trading.
- Major changes in the legal framework are by-products of the *European Single Market*: As was done for banks before, European insurance companies will be granted easier market access, while they will remain subject to supervision in their home countries. In the next legislative period, the directive on securities services and the Capital Adequacy Directive will have to be implemented into national law.

Service sector liberalisation

- Concerning *transportation*, the capacity for long distance road goods transport has been extended within the existing system of quotas on licences. Binding tariffs for goods transport have been abolished as of 1994 for all means of transport. Deregulation, initiated by the EU, has liberalised market access in air transport. The reform of the Federal Railways (1994) relieves the railways from capital costs and increases the opportunities for market-oriented management decisions.
- Concerning *telecommunications and postal services* the "Postreform II" will give the management of the newly-established joint-stock companies more independence from political influence.
- Concerning *energy policy,* plans to introduce competition to the electricity and gas sectors have been announced. The Bundestag approved a law, which limits future subsidies for coal-mining to DM 7.5 billion in 1996 and to DM 7 billion

(continued on next page)

(continued)

annually from 1997 until 2000. However, the ''coal-penny'', a surcharge on the electricity bill that subsidises the use of expensive German coal in electricity production, has been increased by 1 percentage point to 8.5 per cent in western Germany as of 1994 and will be introduced at half that rate in eastern Germany as of 1996.

Deregulation

- *Planning and approvals procedures*: several laws have been enacted to accelerate investment projects (*e.g.* Laws on *Facilitating Investment* and *Land for Housing Construction*, amendments to *Chemical Law* and the *Gene Technology Law*). By the end of the year, a recently installed independent commission of experts will present its proposals to speed up and alleviate planning and approval procedures. Furthermore, the Ministry of Economics has suggested establishing ''project managers'' to co-ordinate the approvals process when several public authorities are involved.
- *Retail sale*: the *Rebates Law* has been modified to give firms more entrepreneurial freedom (still subject to final parliamentary approval); a liberalisation of shop opening hours has been postponed to the next legislative period.
- *Crafts*: while retaining the master craftsman's certificate, liberalisation (as of 1994) will facilitate the exercise of an independent craft and, in addition, enable craftsmen to supply a broader spectrum of services.

Privatisation

Not counting the operations of the Treuhandanstalt, nine public enterprises have been privatised – at least in part – by the federal government during the current legislation period. Up to end of February 1994, privatisation receipts amounted to DM 1.7 billion (Table B1).

Table B.1. **Enterprises privatised by the Federal Government**

Company	Main activity	Total assets in DM
Industrieverwaltungsgesellschaft AG	Industrial holding	663 million
Industrieanlagen-Betriebsgesellschaft mbH	Industrial holding	107 million
Deutsche Pfandbrief- und Hypothekenbank AG	Credit institution	63.4 billion
Berliner Industriebank AG	Credit institution	7.7 billion
C&L Treuarbeit Deutsche Revision AG	Audit company	558 million
Prakla-Seismos AG	Mechanical engineering	312 million
Aachener Bergmannssiedlungsgesellschaft mbH	Real estate company	138 million
Schenker & Co GmbH[1]	Transport	1.4 billion
Deutsche Baurevision AG[1]	Audit company	16 million

1. Partial privatisation (reduction of public equity holdings).
Source: Bundestagsdrucksache 12/6889.

Standort Report on the subject of subsidies is rather vague and subsidy reduction plays a negligible role in the plan for medium-term budget consolidation.

A second prime target of medium and long-term reform is social spending. Projections of population ageing imply that by the year 2030 over 60 per cent of total wage costs would be consumed by social security contributions if there were no policy action to prevent it.[69] The "Rentenreformgesetz 1992" (Old-age pension reform law of 1992) should reduce (by about half) the projected increase in the old-age pension contribution rate by sharing the burden among beneficiaries, contributors, and the federal government. The indexing of old age pensions is now based on the (more moderate) development of net wages instead of gross wages, the pension age are to be raised to 65, and grants by the federal government to the pension funds are now linked to contributions (*i.e.*, they will increase over time). However, further policy action will probably be necessary in the longer run to fully address the population ageing problem while keeping contribution rates at economically efficient levels.

The welfare state is endangered not only by the demographic problem and the rise of unemployment, but also by the evasion of contribution payments and abuse of benefits within the shadow economy. In response to such problems, the government has launched an initiative for a more efficient targeting of social benefits and improved controls in several areas of state activity, as well as some retrenchment of benefit entitlements, tax loopholes and concessions. An interim report has indicated encouraging first results, while further savings measures are still under discussion.[70] Once all proposed measures take full effect, the government estimates that annual savings for the public budgets will be at least DM 20 billion, including DM 8 billion for the federal budget. Even so, the re-establishment of the correct balance between social benefits and the incentive to work remains a lasting task for German politics.

Both social security and labour market reform raise complex distributional problems. However, as seen above, greater inter-sectoral flexibility of wages is an important pre-condition for development of the service sector which in turn is essential to solution of the unemployment problem. Despite recent liberalisation, current job-protection legislation still constitutes an entry barrier, discriminating against the risk-taking small and medium-sized business sector, a bias which could be mitigated by reducing the costs of social plans and raising the minimum size of the firm subject to such legislation. The way should also be cleared for the effective minimum wage to fall to levels that would price low-skilled workers back into the market,[71] which is a recommendation of the Council of Economic Advisers, while to offset the effect of short working hours and lengthen machine run-times, steps should be taken to make shifts and working hours more flexible.[72] Finally, the social partners should be encouraged to explore ways to make the current system of wage bargaining more sensitive to individual firm productivity and profit positions, as suggested in previous *Surveys*.

Opening the service sectors to greater competition

In the telecommunications sector, a "Postreform II" has been regarded as inevitable, including as its main elements the transformation of the three successors of the former Bundespost into joint-stock companies. However, existing monopolies concerning access to network and voice traffic will remain untouched, despite EU plans to liberalise these market segments in the near future. Further doubts that the reform goes far enough focus on the partial approach to privatisation and on a possibly lasting governmental influence on management decisions.[73] It is envisaged that the federal Government will maintain a majority stake in the postal service for at least five years. As for Telekom, an increase in share capital on the capital market – without participation of the federal Government – will reduce the Bund's shareholder position. An institution under public law (Bundesanstalt für Post und Telekommunikation Deutsche Bundespost) will be founded to exercise the ownership functions and to protect the interests of Government. Any cross-subsidisation between one operation and another should be more transparent within this new framework. But the authority of the "Bundesanstalt" will be extended to a critical degree in the field of social affairs, including the conclusion of framework agreements on working standards. Provided that the telecommunications market is opened to new suppliers, Telekom should be given the opportunity to act like all other private market participants, in order to ensure a level playing field in telecommunications and to exploit the potential gains of enhanced competition.

The Council of Economic Advisors has examined different ways of enhancing competition in electricity distribution in a recent report.[74] The first suggestion would oblige the current owners of networks, who are energy producers themselves, to give other producers access to the networks, as long as there is idle capacity. While leaving the vertical integration of existing utilities untouched, (commercial) consumers would have the opportunity to choose the cheapest supplier and more efficient electricity producers (domestic or foreign) would be able to enter the market – both suggestions aimed at stimulating competition in a hitherto uncompetitive environment. The two main problems concern the prior rights to capacity for established utilities and their – potentially unfair – pricing behaviour. The Council thus prefers an alternative, which implies a separation of production, transmission, and final sale of electricity. All energy producers would have competitive access to the grid; the then independent network owners could choose the suppliers by auctioning the existing transmission capacity. End-users would be charged at marginal production cost (plus transmission and distribution). The procedure constitutes not only an incentive to use the most efficient existing power plants but to invest in the most competitive electricity generation technique.

A comprehensive reform of energy distribution would have to surmount a number of economic and legal difficulties: *e.g.* to find an adequate pricing scheme or de-monopolise the vertically integrated utilities. There is also opposition from the Länder and local authorities who are owners of utilities and some of whom run power stations and are threatened by a loss of monopoly rents, income and/or political influence.[75] In the Standort Report, the Government mentioned utilities as potential candidates for privatisation. Given the cost problems of German enterprises, the topic would deserve a higher priority on the political agenda, specifically at the regional and local levels.

The regulatory framework covering distribution could be made more competitive if certain legal provisions were changed. The Monopoly Commission has criticised legal restrictions which could possibly inhibit the establishment of new (land-consuming) shopping centres, or shop opening hours, a topic discussed in former *Surveys*. The Government has postponed any reform steps concerning shop opening hours to the next legislature. Experience with the "long Thursday" (shops are allowed to open on Thursday evening until 8.30 p.m.) will, then, be evaluated. Still in legislation is the reform of the Rebates Law (Rabattgesetz), originally dating from 1933. The abolition of fixed limits for rebates would stimulate greater competition in some retail markets, bringing the law into line with *de facto* practice, if reports on the widespread use of higher-than-allowed rebates are correct.

Supporting a higher level of innovation

Heavier government involvement *per se* would not guarantee successful broad-based innovation. Indeed, if the government were to allocate to itself a large interventionist role the result could be that targeted sectors are shielded from competitive forces or that innovative resources are misdirected. Innovation should thus be fostered primarily by indirect means – an approach which would be consistent with the principles of the Social Market economy. Two areas suggest themselves as requiring attention:

- Promotion of more market-based forms of risk finance through *capital market development*. Recent policy reforms have improved the conditions for stock market access, especially of small and medium sized firms, while also improving market transparency. However, firms still need to make use of the new opportunities, which might include giving greater attention to business management training. Greater expertise may be needed both to encourage further progress in venture capital finance and to prepare young firms for entry into the stock market.

- Promotion of more flexible skills through *general education and training*. The trend toward higher formal attainment within the apprentice population would seem to indicate that the apprenticeship system, in conjunction with the academic system, might be already in the process of finding the appropriate mix between vocational skills and general knowledge. In this way, the youth training system is likely to continue to make an important contribution to the ongoing success of Germany's economy. However, university reform, better career counselling, and less specialisation of training programmes will also be needed to create a better match between skills and final employment opportunities, geared to changing technology.

To compensate for the high costs but economy-wide spillovers from R&D, a case could also be made for greater use of tax incentives to encourage innovation; but these would need to be broad-based to avoid allocational distortions. More immediately, perhaps, there is a need to expedite the project approval process at lower levels of government. While delays often arise, legitimately, from environmental concerns, these would not seem fully to explain the difference between German procedures and those elsewhere.

V. Conclusions

Over the last eighteen months the German economy had to face the challenge of overcoming a recession while continuing the reconstruction process begun by unification. Demand and output in the western part of the country fell by almost 2 per cent in 1993, as receding foreign demand was compounded by negative repercussions of domestic imbalances. Pan-German GDP was on average 1 1/4 per cent lower than in 1992, although output growth remained buoyant in the eastern Länder. Unemployment rose and public finances weakened, but with capacity slack substantial and import prices falling, inflation abated.

While domestic demand remained depressed, the past year has marked a turnaround in the economy, with signs of improvement becoming more visible in recent months. Thus, following a recovery in exports and construction orders in the second half of 1993, industrial activity has started picking up in the west and has reaccelerated in the east. More importantly, the major imbalances and distortions which had contributed to recession have begun to be corrected. Exchange rates have remained broadly stable and German competitiveness has ceased to be undermined by domestic wage pressures. As a consequence of the fall in output and the implicit threat to jobs, wage settlements have been more moderate than expected, mitigating the burden imposed on firms over the past two years, while the timetable for convergence of eastern German wages to western levels has been extended. Seeking to regain lost export shares, firms have embarked on sweeping cost-cutting and rationalisation programmes and intensified marketing efforts, notably in the fast-growing regions outside Europe. In eastern Germany, the base of the expansion has broadened, being now more firmly established in manufacturing output and investment, and the huge gap between demand and output in the new Länder has at last started narrowing. While much remains to be done there has been undeniable progress in reconstructing the industrial base.

117

With the external environment improving and domestic imbalances unwinding, growth of activity is expected to pick up gradually in 1994, reaching 1¾ per cent overall and accelerating to a sustainable medium-term pace of around 2½ per cent in 1995. In the absence of major exchange-rate turbulence, exports will remain the driving force, helped by a stabilisation in cost-competitiveness. With output rising, capacity utilisation in manufacturing will increase and profits should recover; the decline in business fixed investment in the west should thus be reversed, while capital spending should maintain its buoyancy in eastern Germany. Unemployment will, nevertheless, continue rising in 1994, as firms initially increase output by raising productivity, before starting to hire. With labour slack remaining significant, wage growth is likely to stay modest, allowing consumer price inflation to abate to below 2 per cent as from mid-1995. Private consumption will thus be a lagging component in the recovery of domestic demand, especially since the decline in real disposable income in 1994 will be compounded by the re-introduction of the ''solidarity'' income tax surcharge in 1995. With the major contribution to the resumption of GDP growth coming from exports, the current account deficit should shrink markedly to around ¼ per cent of GDP.

The projected gradual but somewhat uneven recovery is contingent upon a strengthening in exports and a fall in the household saving ratio. In these respects, it is subject to a number of negative risks. Thus, the rise in international interest rates might lead to slower export market growth, while upward pressure on the effective Deutschemark rate could imply a renewed drag on German competitiveness. On the domestic side, the risk of unemployment and the squeeze on household incomes could make households more reluctant to draw on their savings. However, recent leading indicators suggest the possibility of greater export buoyancy and, in this event, a stronger than projected pick-up in profits could encourage higher investment. With output remaining below capacity, faster growth is unlikely to generate any price pressures in the short term, but the liquidity overhang from monetary overshooting may pose an inflation risk in the medium term.

Monetary policy has pursued a line of cautious easing, taking the discount rate down to 4½ per cent, more than 4 percentage points below its 1992 peak. Relaxation has been warranted both by progress in disinflation, reflected in historically low bond-market rates, and by the maintenance of a broadly stable

DM/dollar exchange rate. The broad money supply (M3), on the other hand, has significantly exceeded the target range in recent months. There is evidence to suggest that special transitory factors have been largely responsible for the overshooting. The Bundesbank has, in consequence, shown flexibility in the implementation of policy, taking account of other monetary and non-monetary indicators in its decision-making. The recent overshooting could be evidence of an unwanted build-up in liquidity which would signal future inflationary danger. On balance, though, with inflation projected to abate towards the Bundesbank target range of below 2 per cent and no new constraints on capacity or cost pressures in sight, it has been possible to reduce short-term rates. In this respect, the cuts in policy-controlled interest rates announced by the Bundesbank in early May are to be welcomed, while, depending on the extent of monetary decelera-tion, the pace of disinflation and the strength of demand, there may be some further scope for reductions to give support to recovery.

Nevertheless, the large deviation of monetary growth from target raises the question of the appropriateness of the M3 indicator and its reliability for policy. The Bundesbank is assuming that the influence of special factors will disappear over time, and that it is therefore appropriate to maintain M3 as a yardstick, while steering a pragmatic course that tolerates deviations from target when justified by other indicators. This course seems to be justified, since, for the moment, the distortions observed do not necessarily rule out a long-run relationship between the money stock and other major macroeconomic variables, such as prices and growth. Indeed, part of the value of monetary targets is that they oblige the central bank to justify why, in its view, tolerating a deviation from the target will not endanger price stability. A systematic explanation of the nature and causes of deviations from the target could help prevent any erosion of confidence, while securing the appropriate degree of flexibility in the conduct of monetary policy.

Public finances have been under strong pressure from the expenditure side in the wake of reunification, eliciting a marked policy shift towards fiscal restric-tion. The general government deficit widened to $3^{1}/_{4}$ per cent of GDP in 1993, but this was attributable to cyclical factors. The structural (cyclically-adjusted) deficit has been sharply reduced. With economic recovery gaining strength, it should be possible, in conformity with government plans, to lower the general government deficit to around DM 92 billion in 1994 and reduce it further thereafter. A ceiling on public expenditure growth is the main mechanism for achieving this, although consolidation will also depend on higher revenues. Thus, by 1995, when the "solidarity" income tax surcharge will be reintroduced, expenditure and revenues as a share of GDP will be around 5 percentage points higher than before reunification. Even so, the public debt ratio may rise to over 60 per cent as the government, having assumed responsibility for the liabilities of the German railways in 1994, takes over the debt incurred by the Treuhandanstalt.

Looking ahead to the medium term, assuming fiscal slippage can be avoided, the measures adopted so far seem to have put German finances on to a sustainable footing. The general government debt ratio should begin to fall in the second half of the decade. However, government claims on resources, as measured by the overall level of taxation, will remain significantly higher than in the pre-unification period. By distorting efficient allocation and weakening international competitiveness, this could undermine the achievement of the faster medium-term growth which is needed to underpin the fiscal consolidation process, reduce unemployment and successfully cope with the remaining challenges of reunification. A clear and consistent strategy is thus needed for the second half of the decade in order to scale back the public sector and alleviate the fiscal burden. This should entail the phasing out of the "solidarity" tax surcharge, as the transfer requirements of eastern Germany decline. In order to facilitate the creation of new jobs, non-wage labour costs should also be reduced, and for this to be reconciled with budget deficit reduction, public expenditure will need to be contained, attention being concentrated on the cutting of remaining subsidies to non-viable industries and, building on initiatives already undertaken, a better targeting of social benefits. Furthermore, the scaling back of the public sector depends also on sustained budgetary discipline among the states and municipalities, whose collective outlays are one-third larger than those of the federal government. More local services should be privatised and administrative efficiency raised.

While fiscal consolidation should enhance the growth potential of the economy over the medium term, more generally prospects in this regard are somewhat mixed. On the one hand, Germany has maintained a much higher proportion of industrial employment than elsewhere in the OECD and has consolidated its position as the pre-eminent EU exporter of manufactures. Good industrial performance has been based on exploiting proven areas of comparative advantage, with both financial and human capital resources tending to be concentrated on the traditional exporting sectors, mainly in high-quality investment goods. Despite recent losses of global market shares, it may well be that German manufacturing, relying on its traditional strengths, will continue to serve as a motor for economic growth. On the other hand, Germany seems exposed to risks if this pattern cannot be fully realised. The development of the private service sector has been relatively slow, while the diversification to highly innovative, human capital-intensive production has clearly lagged behind that of Germany's main competitors outside Europe. Traditional strengths may thus need to be allied to greater flexibility in adapting the economy to new products and technologies, especially in the service sector.

While unemployment has remained lower than in the rest of Europe, reflecting the comparative strength of the traditional sector, dismissed workers risk remaining unemployed for extended periods because of certain structural rigidities. Inflexible labour markets bear part of the blame: a rigid wage structure that does not adequately reflect inter-firm and inter-sectoral productivity differentials has resulted from a centralised wage-bargaining system. Perhaps most importantly, the contract wage, as *a de facto* minimum wage, has, in many cases, priced low-skilled workers out of the job market. At the same time, high tax rates and unemployment benefits which are generous by international standards have reduced incentives to get back into the labour market, while stiff rules on worker dismissals have undermined the incentives to firms to hire. In these respects there is a need for a legal framework which allows greater flexibility and for the social partners to make use of it. It is encouraging that the law extending the allowable length of fixed-term contracts from six to eighteen months has been recently renewed, the possibilities for part-time work and flexible working times expanded, and employment placement services opened to private firms. Of course, this should go hand in hand with establishing the conditions for more job opportunities. The government might take a lead in this area by promoting greater wage and working time flexibility within the public sector. The social partners should make use of the recently enlarged legal opportunities for longer operating hours, while making working schedules more flexible. They should also work toward greater variability of wages across firms and sectors, as well as toward adjustment of vocational training curricula.

Germany's supply-side strength has also been adversely affected by high costs stemming from impediments to competition and excessive regulation. The wage shock that accompanied the unification boom is now in the process of unwinding, though so far reversing only partially the initial competitiveness losses. Moreover, lack of competition remains a problem in the sheltered sectors, which provide inputs to the tradeables industries. Protected sectors include agriculture, several major service sectors, mining and weak manufacturing sectors such as shipbuilding and steel. A major instrument of protection is subsidies, the cost of which, by one estimate, amounts to around 4 to 5 per cent of GDP, equivalent to the entire transfer burden to eastern Germany. The main instruments of protection in services are long-standing state involvement in transport and communications, restrictive regulations and barriers to market entry. The rules governing opening hours in the retail sector are perhaps the most conspicuous case in point, but further liberalisation is also needed in the areas of insurance, road transport, telecommunications and energy provision. The high costs involved in such rigidities may have had adverse repercussions on employment growth and consumer welfare.

To alleviate supply-side rigidities, the German government has since the mid-1980s committed itself to a programme of deregulation, tax reform, and privatisation. Significant progress has been made and the plan of action has been strengthened in the context of its recent *Standort* Report. Nevertheless, certain gaps in the reform strategy need to be filled. First, although progress has been made in reducing industrial subsidies in western Germany, an immediate action plan for the phasing out of *still*-existing subsidies remains a priority. This would provide greater scope for generalised tax relief, hasten structural reform, and lower inflationary biases in the economy. Although subsidies may be required to facilitate the transition in eastern Germany, these should carry strict time limits for expiration. Tax credits should be maintained only if they are non-discriminatory, as is the case with general credits for R&D. Second, the proposed reforms in the retail sector leave unexploited the openings for part-time employment which liberalisation would provide. This is urgently needed, as disincentives to part-time work are relatively onerous.

Germany could also go farther and faster in privatising and in reducing the many barriers to market entry. For example, the tendency of the western Länder to have major share-holdings in business concerns risks spreading to the eastern Länder and should be reversed through divestitures of all existing properties linked with business activities. The federal government also needs to assume a more forceful leadership role in the creation of a more friendly regulatory environment for innovative activity. Many barriers to new activities – both explicit regulations and bureaucratic inertia – have very little basis in either economic or scientific logic. The Bund needs to set national standards and guidelines to speed up plant approval procedures and facilitate scientific research, and it must do so urgently as world developments in the new technology areas are proceeding at a rapid rate. Further development of the corporate capital market, vocational training and university reform, are likewise needed to ensure an adequate supply of resources to the new growth areas. This should not, however, comprise direct support to so-called strategic sectors. Experience shows that government intervention in the high-tech area often backfires, and that firms tend to develop a dependency on government assistance rather than using it as a springboard to change.

Implementation of reforms along these lines would go a long way towards strengthening the German "model" of the social-market economy. It is all the more important because constructing a market economy in the eastern Länder is essential to reducing the burden on productive resources in the west. Unification should thus be taken as an opportunity for invigorating the forces of entrepreneurship and innovation. Doing so would not only shorten the horizon and lower the costs of completing economic reunification, but also help to secure Germany's future economic success and social stability.

Notes and references

1. While the year-on-year decline narrowed steadily during the year, it was still close to 1 per cent in the fourth quarter.

2. Thus, the sharpness of the downturn in neighbouring European countries was partly due to the waning of spill-over effects from the positive German demand shock; moreover, the "displacement" effect of foreign by eastern German demand may have been largest in the immediate aftermath of the establishment of monetary union and is now being reversed, as local productive capacity is being built up in eastern Germany.

3. The only case of the savings ratio going up during a recession was in 1975, which is occasionally taken as evidence for "Angst" saving. However, even in this case the rise may be explained by the abnormally high income growth of that year, caused by "wrong" signals emanating from forecasting errors for wage negotiations, tax cuts and other special factors.

4. The profit/earnings ratio of 6 per cent in 1993 compares with a historical low of 2.1 per cent in 1982.

5. Eastern German GDP per employee as a percentage of the western German level moved up from 28 per cent to 46 per cent. However, large price differentials between east and west still distort the comparison of value added (contribution to GDP) in sectors like housing or transportation. About half of the catching-up in per capita GDP may be attributed to the above-average price rises in the east, according to the German statistical office.

6. In fact, current transfers account for about 25 per cent of household disposable income in the west, but for more than 40 per cent in the east.

7. The so-called "wage quota" – the amount of national income devoted to wages and salaries – remains at over 100 per cent, implying no profits are being generated.

8. However, in both categories, services and housing costs, inflation has notably slowed since mid-1993.

9. For seven to fifteen-year bonds.

10. *Deutsche Bundesbank Annual Report, 1993*, April 1994, p. 26.

11. However, low capital formation understates the propensity to acquire long-term financial assets, as the introduction of a 30 per cent withholding tax on interest income in January 1993 prompted German residents to shift financial assets into mutual funds based in Luxembourg.

12. The introduction of a 30 per cent withholding tax on interest income earned by domestic residents in January 1993 triggered major shifts of financial assets into mutual funds in neighbouring Luxembourg and large-scale hoarding of banknotes towards the end of 1992. However, a large part of the funds shifted abroad flowed back to the German capital market through investment purchases, so that this did not constitute any burden on long-term interest rates or the exchange rate. In January 1994, the withholding tax was extended to accrued interest on German holdings in foreign-based investment funds, when realised through corresponding capital gains, which triggered a repatriation of offshore funds held in Luxembourg as these instruments lost appeal. Cash realised through these transactions failed to return to the bond market because of turbulent conditions and a turn upwards in long-term interest rates.

13. There were sizeable outflows of funds in domestic non banks' external payments transactions after the speculative inflows in autumn 1992. In addition, currency in circulation, which had been bloated by the introduction of the tax on interest income, declined sharply.

14. Deutsche Bundesbank, *Monthly Report*, February 1994, p. 8.

15. See Deutsche Bundesbank, "The correlation between monetary growth and price movements in the Federal Republic of Germany", *Monthly Report*, January 1992, pp. 20-28.

16. DIW, "Schlechte Absatzlage bewirkt Gewinneinbrüche", *Wochenbericht* 10/94, pp. 133-139.

17. See OECD, *Economic Survey on Germany*, Paris 1993, Chapter III, "Public Finances after Unification".

18. The state of public finances is monitored using two different statistical records:

    i) the net credit demand of the territorial authorities on a financial basis, which covers the federal government, the Länder and local authorities and the various federal funds; and

    ii) the general government deficit, on a national accounts basis, which includes the social security system in addition to the territorial authorities.

19. The Programme amounts to DM 21 billion for the federal government, including the Federal Labour Office, and to DM 26 billion for the general government as a whole in 1994. By 1996 the savings are expected to amount to DM 25 billion for the federal government and DM 34 billion for the general government.

20. This calculation is based on a series of crude assumptions, concerning in particular the choice of the discount rate, supposed to move back progressively to the real long-term interest rate average since 1800. A 1.5 per cent increase, which would keep the discount rate more in line with recent trends, would reduce net commitments but they would still be high – around 125 per cent of GDP. (*Source*: Paul van den Noord and Richard Herd, "Pension Liabilities in the Seven Major Countries", OECD Economics Department *Working Papers*, No. 142, 1993.)

21. See DIW, "Bundesrepublik Deutschland: Strukturkrise oder konjunktureller Einbruch?", *Wochenbericht*, 26-27/93, pp. 360-368.

22. See Bundesministerium für Wirtschaft, "Zukunftssicherung des Standortes Deutschland", Bonn, 1993.

23. For most of the analysis, "Germany" refers to the former Federal Republic of Germany. The structural problems of eastern Germany are in most cases of a totally different nature, and will not be treated here (see *Annual Survey of Germany*, 1990, 1991, 1992 and 1993 issues).

24. The substitution of labour by capital was induced by sharp real wage increases in the early 1970s and again in the early 1990s. Immigration (a growth factor generally more important than in other countries) also declined sharply between 1973 and 1989.

25. Estimates of the NAIRU (non-accelerating-inflation rate of unemployment) show an increase from 1-2 per cent in the early 1970s to 5.5-9.0 per cent in the 1980s, and the "MURU" (mean-utilisation rate of unemployment – perhaps a better proxy of the natural rate of unemployment given that the rate of capacity utilisation may be a more important direct determinant of inflation than the unemployment rate) is estimated to have grown from 1 per cent in 1970 to 8 per cent in 1990. See Franz, R. and R.J. Gordon, "German and American wage and price dynamics: Differences and common themes", *European Economic Review*, Vol. 37, No. 4, May 1993, pp. 719-754.

26. See Giersch, H., K-H. Paqué, and H. Schmieding, *The Fading Miracle, Four decades of market economy in Germany*, Cambridge University Press, 1992, who state that after the mid-1970s, structural unemployment was "the one major macroeconomic deficiency that overshadowed everything else", (p. 195).

27. Giersch *et al., op cit.*

28. It has been estimated that unemployment alone was responsible for about $\frac{1}{2}$ percentage point of the growth slowdown after 1973. See Maddison, A., "Growth and Slowdown in Advanced Capitalist Economies: Techniques of Qualitative Assessment", *The Journal of Economic Literature*, Vol. 25, No. 2, June 1987, pp. 649-698.

29. In 1990, Germany alone accounted for 31 per cent of EC manufacturing output. See Commission of the European Communities, "Market Services and European integration, the challenges for the 1990s", *European Economy, Social Europe*, No. 3, 1993.

30. To the extent that Germany may record as manufacturing production certain activities that other countries regard as services, for example as a consequence of the growing trend in these countries toward out-sourcing of service-type parts of the manufacturing process, the noted discrepancies in the relative size of the manufacturing sector could be overstated.

31. Average annual growth of investment volume of services was 2.7 per cent during the 1980s, compared with 6.6 per cent in the United States and 5.1 per cent in Japan.

32. There was at the same time a rise in employment in the state and non-profit private sector of around $1\frac{1}{2}$ million.

33. To a large extent, the shift of production to eastern Germany was accomplished *via* a rise in the exchange rate, hence a reduction in competitiveness, so that the different causes of market share loss are not mutually exclusive.

34. The measurement of export market shares in 1993 may be distorted by the abolition of EC customs barriers as of 1 January, which resulted in an under-reporting of exports and imports for all EC countries. Since the under-reporting of imports is believed to have been greater than that of exports, the bias in measurement of export performance could even have been in the upward direction.

35. Levels here are obtained by linking growth rates to a 1987 benchmark. The use of value added per hour to measure sectoral productivity may not be as good as output per hour because the latter captures the effects of service and energy prices on competitiveness. Another problem is the use of unit values, rather than prices, to compare levels in the benchmark year. Nonetheless, the basic implications remain valid. See Jorgensen, D., comments to van Ark, B. and D. Pilat, "Productivity Levels in Germany, Japan and the United States: Differences and Causes", *Brookings Papers: Microeconomics 2*, 1993, pp. 1-69. Also see *Manufacturing Productivity*, McKinsey Global Institute, Washington D.C., October 1993.

36. See van Ark and Pilat, *op cit.*

37. While, *a priori*, high concentration should also have been an advantage from the point of view of innovation insofar as high costs of development can be shared and high risks can be pooled in a concentrated industry setting, over-concentration could also reflect a resistance to structural change and barriers to entry of smaller, innovative, and risk-taking firms.

38. There could also be a cross-country measurement problem insofar as German manufacturing sector statistics might include service-type activities that other countries exclude (see footnote 30 above).

39. As will be seen below, this does not necessarily mean that German firms *per se* are weak in such areas, but rather than R&D is often undertaken by German firms in laboratories located in other countries. Also, Germany does excel in environmental products, perhaps as a by-product of stiff environmental regulations, which could be an important "sector of the future". See Frankel M., "Germany's international competitive position under siege", *Inter-economics*, Vol. 29, No.1, January/February 1994, pp. 10-17.

40. For example, problems in sectoral classifications are well-known: products classified as medium-tech (such as cars) may contain many custom-built high-tech inputs (such as semiconductors). On the other hand, insofar as such inputs are produced in Germany, this would be captured in the revealed comparative advantage for high-tech products.

41. See *Annual Survey of Germany*, July 1988, for an earlier discussion of some of these supply-side constraints. Also see OECD, *Assessing Structural Reform: Lessons for the Future*, 1994, for a more recent review of structural policies.

42. Collective bargaining takes place between highly centralised trade unions and employers' federations. The system is often referred to as "corporatism". In manufacturing and mining, sector-wide wage bargaining proceeds by region, but the vast majority of agreements follow the pattern set by a few "pilot" agreements negotiated by the powerful metal-workers' union. Actual wage increases are often higher than centrally negotiated increases due to wage drift at the firm level achieved through a system of bonuses. During recessions, negative wage drift is possible by the retraction of bonuses, and by the disproportionate laying-off of expensive older workers. In recent years, shorter working hours and other working conditions (such as the delaying of introduction of labour-saving technologies, *e.g.*, in the printing sector) have played an increasing role in wage negotiations. In services, the pattern is set by the public sector negotiations, which are nation-wide. Even though less than 40 per cent of the work force is unionised, and only 80 per cent of enterprises are represented in employers' associations, labour law prohibits differential treatment of union and non-union labour, so

that two-thirds of the work force is covered by the results of collective bargaining; also, contract wages are to be regarded as minimum wages (there is no legislated minimum wage). See Carruth, A. and C. Schnabel, "The determination of contract wages in west Germany", *Scandinavian Journal of Economics,* Vol. 95, No. 3, 1993, pp. 297-310.

See OECD *Employment Outlook* 1993, pp. 157-184, and Dreze, J.H. and E. Malinvaud, "Growth and employment: the scope for a European initiative", in *European Economy* 1/1994, pp. 77-106.

Macroeconomic studies of nominal wage behaviour in Germany show that wage moderation is very cyclical and fades away after about three or four years in the process of recovery, no matter how large the remaining labour surplus turns out to be. See Blanchard O. and L. Summers, "Hysteresis and the European unemployment problem", *NBER Macroeconomics Annual,* Vol. 1, 1986, pp. 15-78. Also see Coe, D. and T. Kreuger, "Why is unemployment so high at full capacity? The persistence of unemployment, the natural rate, and potential output in the Federal Republic of Germany", *IMF Working Paper* No. 101, Washington, D.C. October 1990.

The empirical evidence depends to some extent on the indicators used. Whereas the *relative difference* in hourly earnings was in fact decreasing between 1975 and 1992, the *coefficient of variation* (standard deviation divided by arithmetic average) was broadly unchanged until 1991 and decreased only somewhat in 1992. See Sachverständigenrat zur Begutachtung der gesamtwirtschaftlichen Entwicklung, Zeit zum Handeln – Antriebskräfte stärken, *Jahresgutachten* 1993/94, pp. 247-249.

Though this law was originally intended to expire in 1995, it has been recently extended until the year 2000.

See Held, A., "Deregulierung in Deutschland", HWWA *Wirtschaftsdienst,* 1993/IV, Hamburg, pp. 215-220.

For the next three years the current workforce is protected against dismissals. See Kwasniewski, K., Reform der Bahnpolitik, HWWA *Wirtschaftsdienst* 1993/XII, pp. 610-611.

European Commission, "Growth, Competitiveness, Employment", *White Paper,* 1993, p. 79. The Commission has meanwhile modified its position with regard to open access.

For details see Sondergutachten der Monopolkommission, *Marktstruktur und Wettbewerb im Handel,* February 1994.

See European Commission, *European Economy, Social Europe (1993), op cit.* and "Growth, Competitiveness, Employment", *White Paper,* 1993, p. 80.

As noted in Table 33, cash grants by the Länder and municipalities are not included in this estimate due to problems with data collection.

The degree of "effective subsidisation", *i.e.* the total value of subsidies relative to value added, is estimated by one source at almost 10 per cent in the mid-1980s (see Giersch *et al.,* 1992, *ibid.,* pp. 222-236). In international terms, German subsidies as a proportion of GDP were estimated to be about $1/2$ percentage point higher than the EC average prior to unification (see EC, *Third survey on State aids,* 1992); according to internal OECD calculations, these relationships have changed little since then, apart from the above-noted partial shift of subsidisation within Germany from west to east.

54. Innovations occur through three channels: 1) basic research, conducted in university or private institute setting, but usually heavily supported by government due to its clear-cut "public good" aspect; 2) development, or the application of basic research to marketable products, conducted by industry often with government subsidisation, but driven by a clear profit motive; 3) learning-by-doing productivity innovations, *i.e.* new ideas and techniques developed in the normal course of productive activity. This section focuses on the second form of innovation.

55. New equity issues in the German stock market doubled during the second half of the last decade and tripled in the early nineties, if compared with the annual issuance level up to the early eighties. During the same time the number of joint-stock companies listed on the stock exchange increased by more than 15 per cent.

56. The German company sector comprises more than 2 million firms of which less than 3 thousand are joint stock companies, and only some 500 are listed on the stock exchange.

57. See Eston, J.A., "Firm ownership structure and investment: theory and evidence from German panel data", *Wissenschaftszentrum* Berlin, July 1993 (unpublished). This paper shows that firms with close banking ties are less liquidity constrained than those without such ties, thus having a higher propensity to invest.

58. The Max Planck Gesellschaft, the leading scientific research institute in Germany, as well as other scientific organisations, warn that as a result of regulatory system, basic research in Germany is steadily backtracking. See Lux, A., "Die Wettbewerbsposition Deutschlands in der neuen Biotechnologie", *Wirtschaftsdienst,* 1993/VII, pp. 369-374.

59. Lux, *op. cit.*

60. Steedman, H., "The Economics of Youth Training in Germany", *The Economic Journal,* Vol. 103, No. 420, September 1993. pp. 1279-91.

61. Placements range from prestigious banking firms – who recruit almost exclusively 19-year olds that have completed the rigorous university entrance exam (or Abitur) – to butchers and bakers who recruit 16-year olds who have at least passed the obligatory nine years of schooling.

62. The 17-year old age cohort peaked in 1981 and has declined continuously since then.

63. Lynch, L., *Strategies for Workplace Training: Lessons from Abroad,* Monograph Economic Policy Institute, Washington D.C., 1993.

64. From 1977 to 1992, first-year student numbers increased 76 per cent. The total enrolment of 22 to 25-year olds in university education, at 14.7 per cent, is significantly higher than the OECD average of 8.8 per cent. For 26 to 29-year olds, the German enrolment was 9.3 per cent, as compared with an OECD average of 3.5 per cent. See *Times Higher Education Supplement,* 2 July 1993.

65. In 1977 it took an average of 5.2 years to obtain a university degree while students graduated from Fachhochschule after 3.8 years. In 1990, the average for universities had risen to 6.7 years and to 5.0 years for Fachhochschule. See HIS *Kurzinformation,* April 1994, Hanover.

66. See Zeitgespräch, "Wie sollte die Hochschulpolitik reformiert werden?", *Wirtschaftsdienst* 1994/V, pp. 223-233.

67. This includes a reform of the curricula, the right to sit again for examinations for those students that apply for the exam after the minimum studying time, and tuition charges for students not having passed their examinations after a fixed number of semesters.

68. In 1991, the Deregulation Committee presented a detailed report proposing over 100 deregulation measures. Since 1992, about 60 of these have been either adopted or legislation has been put forward to implement them.

69. By that time, the ratio of retired people to the active population will have reached 74 per cent, against 36 per cent currently. See Burger, S. and L. Funk, "Soziale Sicherung bei schrumpfender Bevölkerung", *Orientierungen zur Wirtschafts- und Gesellschaftspolitik*, 59 (March 1994), Ludwig-Erhard-Stiftung, Bonn, pp. 37-42.

70. Three major success areas are: 1) by reducing tax concessions, closing tax loopholes, and intensifying periodic tax examinations, additional tax receipts of about DM 11½ billion were realised in 1993; 2) special efforts to fight illegal employment and more controls to check entitlements of unemployment benefits by the Federal Labour Office reduced expenses by DM 1.6 billion; and 3) a better targeting of social benefits, when fully in effect, is estimated to save about DM 3½ billion.

71. A "negative income tax" has also been suggested in some quarters as a way of allowing the minimum wage to fall to below the socially accepted minimum income level, which has been guaranteed by a recent decision of the constitutional court. See Hüther, M., "Ansatzpunkte für einen Umbau des Sozialstaats", *Wirtschaftsdienst*, 1994/III, pp. 127-135.

72. Steps have been already taken in this direction with the recent passage of the Law on Working Times (Arbeitszeitrechtsgesetz), which makes working schedules more flexible.

73. Sachverständigenrat, *Jahresgutachten* 1993/94, pp. 258-259.

74. Sachverständigenrat, *op. cit.* pp. 254-256.

75. For an extensive discussion, see Sachverständigenrat, *op. cit.* p. 256. Methods to tackle the pricing problems and to enhance competition can be found in International Energy Agency, *Utility Pricing and Access: Competition for Monopolies*, OECD, Paris 1991.

Stability of money demand after unification

Introduction

The overshooting of the Bundesbank target range for the growth of M3 has raised questions about the stability of M3, even after correcting for special factors such as currency intervention and the introduction of the withholding tax. In the 1993 OECD *Economic Survey of Germany*, a money demand function was estimated and the issue of its stability was discussed in some detail. Evidence for a stable demand for money relationship in the pre-unification period was presented in so far as it was not possible to reject the proposition that the shift in money demand was once-and-for-all and that the underlying relationship between money and income growth remains broadly unchanged.

In the light of four quarters of new data, the present annex provides a reassessment of the evidence presented up to the end of 1993. Using a slightly re-specified equation, a simplified money demand equation was estimated for the pre-unification period. The results of tests of parameter stability when including the post-unification period are broadly unchanged from last year's *Survey* and no conclusive evidence of structural shift in the long-term relationship between monetary growth and inflation could be found. The power of the tests is, however, still very low and the results should therefore be regarded as tentative.

The "error-correction" model

In line with the 1993 Survey, the following error-correction model was postulated:[1]

$$\Delta m_t = \alpha_1 + \alpha_2 \Delta m_{t-1} + \alpha_3 \Delta p_t + \alpha_4 \Delta y_t + \alpha_5 \Delta IRS_t + \alpha_6 \Delta IRL_t + \alpha_7 EC_{t-1} + e_t$$

$$EC_{t-1} = \beta_1 y_{t-1} + \beta_3 IRS_{t-1} + \beta_4 IRL_{t-1} - (m - p)_{t-1}$$

where m, y and p are natural logarithms of M3, real GDP and the GDP deflator while IRS and IRL are the 3-month interbank rate, and 7 to 15-year government bond yields, respectively. The subscript "t" indicates the period and "Δ" designates time differences and e_t is an error term. The long-term relationship is represented by the "error-correction" term (EC_{t-1}) and price homogeneity is imposed by requiring the coefficients on m and p to be equal but of opposite signs.[2]

In the pre-unification period,[3] the model gives quite plausible coefficient estimates for most variables: an increase in nominal and real income or a cut in short-term rates interest rates would raise money demand both in the short and in the long run. Moreover, the estimated long-term income elasticity is slightly above unity and is highly significant.

Table A.1. **Money demand before and after unification**[1]

A. Pre-unification (estimation period: 1970 Q1 to 1990 Q4)

$$[1.1] \quad \Delta m_t = -1.9^* + 0.09\Delta m_{t-1} + 0.11\Delta p_t + 0.11^*\Delta y_t - 0.12\Delta IRS_t + 0.08^{***}EC_{t-1}$$
$$\qquad\qquad\quad (1.8) \qquad\quad (0.8) \qquad (0.9) \qquad (-1.7) \qquad (3.0)$$

$$EC_{t-1} = 1.07^{***}y_{t-1} - 2.85^{**}IRL_{t-1} - (m-p)_{t-1}$$
$$\qquad\quad (5.7) \qquad\qquad (-2.6)$$

$$R^2 = 0.53$$

$$SEE = 6.3 \times 10^{-3}$$

Lagrange multiplier test of fourth order residual serial correlation: $\chi^2(4) = 3.9$ [0.41]

B. Pre- and post-unification (estimation period: 1970 Q1 to 1993 Q4)

$$[1.2] \quad \Delta m_t = -2.00^{**} - 0.06\Delta m_{t-1} + 0.01\Delta p_t + 0.09\Delta y_t - 0.10\Delta IRS_t + 0.10^{***}EC_{t-1}$$
$$\qquad\qquad\quad (-2.0) \quad (-1.2) \qquad\quad (0.1) \qquad (1.5) \qquad (-1.4) \qquad\quad (-3.6)$$
$$\qquad\qquad + 0.01^{**}DUMMY + 0.12^{***}\Delta DUMMY$$
$$\qquad\qquad\quad (2.6) \qquad\qquad\quad (15.1)$$

$$EC_{t-1} = 1.02^{***}y_{t-1} - 2.94^{***}IRL_{t-1} - (m-p)_{t-1}$$
$$\qquad\quad (5.9) \qquad\qquad (-3.2)$$

$$R^2 = 0.86$$

$$SEE = 6.2 \times 10^{-3}$$

Lagrange multiplier test of up to fourth order residual serial correlation: $\chi^2(4) = 4.7$ [0.32]

F-statistic for structural stability of all coefficients except the constant term: F (7, 77) = 0.64 [0.72][2]

Wald statistic for structural stability of the "long-term" relationship between (m – p), y and IRL: $\chi^2(3) = 1.8$ [0.40].[3]

---

1. T-ratios are indicated in parentheses; square brackets indicate p-values.
   * means "significant at the 10 per cent level".
   ** means "significant at the 5 per cent level".
   *** means "significant at the 1 per cent level".
2. Test of the hypothesis of parameter constancy against the alternative hypothesis of a structural break in 1991 Q1 (p-value in square brackets).
3. Test of parameter constancy in the "error-correction" term (EC_{t-1}).

Tests on, for example, residual serial correlation indicates that the model is quite well specified as the null hypothesis of uncorrelated normally distributed residuals with equal standard deviation cannot be rejected. However, an improved equation (Table A1, equation [1.1]) was obtained by eliminating the two least significant interest rate terms: the change in long-term interest rates (ΔIRL) and the lagged level of short-term interest rates (IRS_{t-1}). Such a simplification provides improved parameter estimates of other variables, in particular the other interest rate terms, and slightly improved specification test statistics.

Structural stability

Having obtained a relatively well specified equation for the pre-unification period, the question of structural stability of the equation in the post-unification period was tested. These tests were performed by analysing the sensitivity of the parameter estimates to an extension of the estimation period to the post-unification period. Two simple dummies were included (DUMMY[4] and ΔDUMMY[5]) in order to correct for any once-and-for-all change in the level of desired money holdings.

The result of extending the estimation period to the post-unification period is reported in equation [1.2]. The impact of the unification on desired money holdings is clear: both the shift dummy (DUMMY) and the impulse dummy (ΔDUMMY) are quite large and highly significant. The parameter estimates of long-term income and interest elasticities are, however, very close to the pre-unification estimates, suggesting no fundamental change in the underlying relationship between money growth, nominal income growth and a change in interest rates.

Formal tests of the stability of the long-run relationship support this impression. The tests were carried out by including a set of dummy variables allowing for a structural break in 1991 Q1 in the long-term relationship (the EC-term). A joint test of the exclusion of these variables could not be rejected, nor could the exclusion of any single of these variables. The power of the test performed on the post-unification period is, however, very low due to the short period of observation. In particular, it is difficult to reject the hypothesis of structural stability of the long-run relationships, being calculated as ratios of the original estimates.

The medium-term effect of the unification shock on the monetary relationships can be illustrated by using the equation to forecast monetary growth towards the year 2000 (Table A.2). The forecast is based on projections of real GDP, inflation and interest rates as set out in the Secretariat's medium-term reference scenario (see Annex II). According to the model, monetary growth is likely to exceed 6 per cent until 1995 and 5½ per cent until 1999, in spite of an assumption of a slow recovery and inflation stabilising at around

Table A.2. **Dynamic forecast: 1994-2000** [1]

Per cent annual growth

	Average		Forecast						
	1980-90	1991-93	1994	1995	1996	1997	1998	1999	2000
M3	5.7	8.0	6.9	6.1	6.0	6.0	6.1	5.8	5.4
Nominal GDP	5.0	5.9	4.6	4.6	4.7	5.1	5.4	5.2	5.0
Velocity [2]	-0.7	-2.1	-2.3	-1.5	-1.3	-0.9	-0.6	-0.6	-0.4

1. Based on equation [1.2] and Secretariat medium-term projections of real GDP, inflation and interest rates.
2. Velocity = $\frac{\text{Nominal GDP}}{\text{M3}}$

Source: OECD.

2 per cent. As a result of the unification shock, the decrease in velocity – *i.e.* the difference between monetary growth and nominal income growth – jumps to a very high level in 1991-94 and stabilises gradually, though not completely, by the turn of the century.[6]

Notes

1. The specification differs from the "error-correction" model presented in the 1993 Survey by substituting the constructed opportunity cost variable ("OC") with short and long-term interest rates.

2. The coefficients, including the coefficients in the EC-term, were all estimated by one-step ordinary least squares (OLS).

3. Although the monetary unification was effective from 1 July 1990, coefficient estimates from the pre-unification period includes data from the two last quarters of 1990, due to the absence of seasonally adjusted all-German figures for the latter half of 1990. Money supply, real GDP and the GDP deflator from western Germany were used for this period.

4. Defined as 0 from 1970 Q1 to 1990 Q4 and 1 thereafter.

5. $\Delta DUMMY(t) = DUMMY(t) - DUMMY(t - 1)$.

6. The trend decrease in velocity – consistent with equation [2.1] – is about –0.3 per cent, given 3 per cent annual growth in potential GDP and 2 per cent inflation.

Annex II

Fiscal consolidation scenarios

To explore the constraints involved in the setting of German fiscal policy over the coming years, the Secretariat has elaborated a number of macroeconomic scenarios for the period 1995-2000. Incorporating the measures decided in the fiscal consolidation programme, a reference scenario has been constructed assessing the evolution of public debt assuming a 3 per cent trend real growth and a 2 per cent inflation (Table A3). An alternative scenario has also been elaborated, to test the sensitivity of the results to changing assumptions about nominal growth. It should be emphasized that these scenarios are not forecasts but conditional projections intended to complement the more stylistic presentation in Diagram 18.

The baseline scenario takes into account the measures already agreed in connection with the Solidarity Pact, with current spending of the territorial authorities rising by no more than 3 per cent in nominal terms. Meanwhile, it is assumed that social welfare spending may grow somewhat faster than 3 per cent, due in particular to the introduction in 1995 of a compulsory long-term care insurance (for a cost estimated at DM 15 billion the first year) and the catch-up process in eastern German social entitlements. In this context, GDP growth is projected to accelerate progressively to 3 per cent per annum from 1997 onwards, supported mainly by a favourable external environment and by investment demand. This combination of sustained medium-term growth and active programmes of fiscal consolidation would be sufficient to achieve an average net lending/ GDP ratio of just over 2 per cent and a debt to GDP of around 60 per cent by the end of the projection period.

Looking at a more conservative growth assumption – a reduction of output growth by a constant ½ per cent per annum relative to the medium term baseline throughout the projection period – illustrates the problems that could emerge from a weaker recovery. This is reflected in lower revenues and higher social transfer payments as well as increased interest payments as the deterioration in fiscal balances feeds through cumulatively into the stock of interest bearing debt. Government total net lending remains slightly above 3 per cent throughout the period, undoing the impact of the medium-term consolidation efforts assumed in the reference scenario. The public debt, instead of falling below 60 per cent of GDP, rises to around 65 per cent by 2000. To offset the slippage resulting from the lower growth assumption, expenditure growth has to be curbed further. A 0.3 per cent reduction in expenditure to GDP ratio (around DM 10 billion in

Table A.3. **Scenarios for medium-term consolidation**

Per cent – 1995-2000

	1995	Average 1996-1999	2000
1. Reference scenario			
Real GDP growth	2.6	3.1	3.0
Real short-term interest rate	2.3	2.2	2.4
Real long-term interest rate	4.1	3.7	3.7
Net lending (per cent of GDP)	–2.8	–2.2	–1.5
Primary balance (per cent of GDP)	+1.8	+2.3	+2.8
General government gross debt (per cent of GDP)	63	61	59
Revenue-to-GDP ratio (per cent of GDP)	47.7	46.4	45.4
2. Low growth scenario (no policy change)			
Real GDP growth	2.1	2.6	2.5
Real short-term interest rate	2.3	2.2	2.4
Real long-term interest rate	4.1	3.7	3.7
Net lending (per cent of GDP)	–3.0	–3.1	–3.2
Primary balance (per cent of GDP)	+1.6	+1.7	+1.6
General government gross debt (per cent of GDP)	63	64	65
Revenue-to-GDP ratio (per cent of GDP)	47.7	46.4	45.4
Memorandum items:			
Tax increase/expenditure cut needed to stabilise the debt ratio at 63 per cent		0.3	

Source: OECD estimates.

1995 prices) would be necessary to stabilise the debt/GDP ratio at its 1995 level by the end of 1997.

A number of lessons emerge from this exercise:

– First, as noted in the text, under present medium-term guidelines, the recovery would be sufficient to eliminate the risk of a debt-interest "snowball", with the debt/GDP ratio converging to the 60 per cent criterion laid down in the Maastricht Treaty.

– Second, the consolidation efforts, although significant, would leave no room to lower the high tax burden. Current receipts would stand at 45½ per cent of GDP by the end of the decade, 1½ point above the pre-unification levels.

– Third, slower growth than that assumed could prevent any reduction in the debt burden, leaving the debt/GDP ratio above the 60 per cent criterion.

Supporting material to Part IV

Table A.4. **Comparison of value added per joint unit of labour and capital by major branch in manufacturing, 1950-90**

Branch	1950[1]	1960	1973	1979	1990
	United States = 100				
Germany/United States					
Food, beverages, tobacco	70.7	83.9	59.1	63.2	64.7
Textiles, apparel, leather	53.7	77.0	70.5	73.5	72.2
Chemicals, allied products	39.6	73.1	99.5	113.1	86.1
Basic, fabricated metals	36.3	61.0	67.4	88.0	101.2
Machinery, equipment	49.8	85.6	94.5	111.9	89.7
Other manufacturing	49.1	67.1	71.2	79.2	76.2
Total manufacturing	47.9	75.0	81.5	95.1	86.2
	Japan = 100				
Germany/Japan					
Food, beverages, tobacco	100.4	112.0	92.2	109.7	137.1
Textiles, apparel, leather	157.0	175.4	119.3	122.5	146.2
Chemicals, allied products	110.3	116.4	120.0	125.4	92.8
Basic, fabricated metals	208.6	250.0	98.1	107.8	107.5
Machinery, equipment	374.4	297.2	148.8	125.2	70.9
Other manufacturing	212.6	217.9	144.4	155.3	128.9
Total manufacturing	155.0	187.0	127.9	133.5	101.3

1. 1955 for Japan.
Source: Van Ark and Pilat *op. cit.*

Table A.5. Non-defence R&D expenditure

	Germany	Japan	United States
	Billions of constant US dollars		
1971	10.1	13.2	41.8
1979	14.2	21.1	52.4
1988	19.9	42.0	78.4
	Percentage increase		
1971-79	40.6	59.8	25.4
1979-88	40.1	99.1	49.6

Source: National Science Board, 1991, *Science and Engineering Indicators – 1991*, NSB91-1, Washington D.C., Government Printing Office.

Table A.6. Corporate finance structure

Average 1989-92; per cent of financial resources

	United States	Japan	France	Italy	Canada	United Kingdom[1]	Germany[2]
Self-finance	79.7	43.6	52.9[3]	51.2	55.1	45.0	60.5
Equity issues	−0.3[4]	6.5	11.7	6.3	10.2	11.9	6.0
Debt	20.6	50.0	35.4	42.5	34.7	43.1	33.5
Direct bank borrowing	1.9	22.8	5.7	15.7	6.8	14.4	12.8
Short-term	−6.3	2.0	−0.0	8.8	6.8	14.4	7.3
Long-term	8.2	20.8	5.7	6.9	..	..	5.5
Securities issues	12.8	4.4	11.9	0.3	1.6	11.7	
Bonds	12.3	4.4	−0.7	0.3	7.5	11.7	20.7
Other	0.4	..	12.6	0.0	−5.9	..	
Other debt	5.9	22.7	17.8	26.5	26.3	17.1	
Memorandum item:							
Uses of funds							
Financial investment	19.8	23.3	38.0	38.6	27.4	16.7	33.7
Investment in tangible assets	80.2	76.7	62.0	61.4	72.6	83.3	66.9

1. 1989-1990.
2. West Germany.
3. Excluding transfers of fixed assets.
4. Negative number reflects high level of merger and acquisition activity during this period, when many firms bought back their own stock.

Source: OECD; Deutsche Bundesbank.

138

Table A.7. **Venture capital industry in various countries** [1]

	Number of venture capital enterprises	Total capital of venture capital enterprises (million $)
United States	550	20 000
United Kingdom	110	4 500
Canada	44	1 000
Japan	70	850
France	45	750
Netherlands	40	650
Germany	25	500
Sweden	31	325
Norway	35	185
Denmark	14	120
Ireland	10	100
Australia	11	50

1. As of end-1986.
Source: Estimates by Venture Economics.

Table A.8. **"Big Three"** [1] **bank influence on firms boards**

Industry description	Distribution of directors	Firms with at least one banker (per cent)
Mining	4	18
Energy	5	40
Chemical	11	55
Metal	12	58
Steel	14	48
Electrotechnical	14	53
Construction	17	48
Retailing	23	58
Total	100	

1. Commerzbank, Deutsche Bank, and Dresdner Bank.
Source: Elston, *op. cit.*

139

Table A.9. **Bank ownership percentages of selected firms in Germany**

Firm name	Bank ownership	Per cent of ownership
Daimler Benz AG	Deutsche Bank	28.5
Bayer AG	Banken und Versicherungen	38
Continental Gummi-Werke AG	Deutsche Bank	28.5
Linde AG	Commerzbank CA.	10
Schering AG	Banken und Versicherungen	23
Heidelberger Zement AG	Dresdner Bank	≥25
Didier-Werke AG	Deutsche Bank	≥25
Brau und Brunnen AG	Bayerische Hyp.	≥25
	Dresdner Bank	≥25
Phoenix AG	Deutsche Bank CA.	20
Holsten Brauerei AG	Vereinsbank in Hamburg	≥25
Schubert und Salzer M.fabrik AG	Slater Walker Bank	≥25
Hannoversche Papierfabriken Alfred-Gronau AG	Commerzbank	25
Bavaria-St. Pauli Brauerei AG	Vereins- und Westbank	≥25
Süd-Chemie AG	Bankhaus Aufhäuser	26
Neue Baumwoll-Spinnerei und Weberei Hof AG	Bayerische Vereinsbank	≥25
	Bayerische Hyp.	≥25
Berliner Kindl Brauerei AG	Bank für Brau-Industrie	≥25
Nordzement AG	Holderbank Financiere Glarus	≥50
Vereinigte Schmirgel und Maschinenfabriken AG	Dresdner Bank	≥25
New York Hamburger Gummi-Waren Compagnie AG	Vereins- und Westbank	≥25
Pfersee Kolbermoor AG	Bayerische Vereinsbank	≥25
Vereinigte Werkstätten Für Kunst Im Handwerk AG	Bankhaus Merck, Finck CA.	≥25
Reichelbräu AG	Bayerische Hyp.	≥25
Erste Kulmbacher Actien Brauerei AG	Bayerische Hyp.	≥25
Hasen-Bräu AG	Bayerische Vereinsbank	76
Würzburger Hofbräu AG	Bankhaus Merck, Finck CA.	70
Aktien-Brauerei Kaufbeuren AG	Bayerische Vereinsbank	50.1
Chemische Werke Brockhues AG	Bankhaus B. Metzler Seel	≥25

Source: Commerzbank annual series *Wer gehört zu Wem?* (1991).

Annex IV

Chronology of main economic events

1993

January

The second stage of the rent reform in the new Länder becomes effective. Full adaptation to western German rent legislation is anticipated for mid-1995.

A 30 per cent withholding tax on interest earnings (35 per cent in the case of over-the-counter selling) enters into force. At the same time, the tax-free threshold for interest earnings is raised to DM 6 000 for single persons and DM 12 000 for married couples.

The general VAT rate is increased from 14 to 15 per cent.

Excise taxes on lamps, salt, sugar and tea are abolished as of 1 January 1993.

The German Banking Law and the "Principles Concerning the Capital and Liquidity of Credit Institutions" are adapted to various EC Directives (Second Banking Coordination Directive, Own Funds Directive, Solvency Ratio Directive) as of January 1993. The major objectives of the amendments are to establish a level playing field for banks in the Single Market by harmonising the authorisation and supervision of credit institutions ("European Passport"). Bank capital is uniformly defined and the capital basis is broadened (8 per cent of the weighted risk assets).

February

The Bundesbank lowers the Lombard rate from 9½ to 9 per cent and the discount rate from 8¼ to 8 per cent. In addition, the Central Bank Council decides to reduce the minimum reserve ratios for time deposits (from 4.95 per cent) and for savings deposits (from 4.15 per cent) to a uniform rate of 2 per cent as of 1 March 1993. Furthermore, the Council announces to sell by tender in the open market up to DM 25 billion of liquidity paper (maturities: three, six and nine months) in March.

The pay settlement for western German public sector employees provides for wages to rise by 3 per cent retroactively as of 1 January 1993, with a social component for the lower income brackets. The 3 per cent rise in salaries for civil servants is postponed to 1 May 1993.

March

The Bundesbank lowers the discount rate from 8 to 7½ per cent.

The federal government and Länder reach agreement on a "Federal Consolidation Programme", that includes the following elements:

- The system of revenue sharing between the federal government and Länder is restructured. As of 1995, the new Länder will be integrated into the financial equalisation system.
- In 1993 and 1994, another DM 3.7 billion and DM 5.35 billion, respectively, will flow into the German Unity Fund.
- Debts of the Treuhandanstalt and the Credit Guarantee Fund (about DM 370 billion) and more than half of the eastern German housing sector debt (DM 31 billion) will be transferred to an inherited debt fund in 1995. Interest payments and principal repayment will be borne by federal budget.
- The Treuhand's credit line is extended in 1993 and 1994 to cope with environmental damage and to secure and restructure industrial cores.
- The Reconstruction Loan Corporation programme to promote residential building is replenished to rise from DM 30 billion to DM 60 billion.
- The federal government commits another DM 2 billion to labour market policy in the new Länder in 1993.
- To finance the above measures, the 7.5 per cent solidarity surcharge on income tax is to be reintroduced as of 1995. There are also spending cuts and tax credit reductions amounting to DM 12 billion.

April

The Bundesbank lowers the Lombard rate from 9 to 8½ per cent and the discount rate from 7½ to 7¼ per cent.

May

The Federal Consolidation Programme is approved by the Bundesrat.

June

The Bundestag approves a supplement to the 1993 federal budget. Due to cyclical reasons and support for the new Länder, expenditure will rise by another DM 22½ billion, whereas receipts are estimated to decrease by DM 2 billion, relative to the original budget. The deficit will grow by DM 24½ billion to DM 68½ billion.

July

The Central Bank Council reduces the Lombard rate – in two steps – from 8½ to 7¾ per cent and the discount rate from 7¼ to 6¾ per cent. Furthermore, the Bundesbank reaffirms the monetary target for 1993, which provides for a 4½ to 6½ per cent expansion of the money stock M3 during the year.

The Bundesrat approves the "Standortsicherungsgesetz", which includes the second stage of a corporation tax reform (coming into effect at the beginning of 1994). Rates of income and corporation tax on business profits are reduced, while some tax concessions as well as possibilities of abuse are to be eliminated.

Old age benefits are increased by 3.86 per cent in western Germany and by 14.24 per cent in eastern Germany.

August

The federal government approves a report on the development of subsidies (14. Subventionsbericht). At the level of the federal state, subsidies are expected to amount to DM 37.6 billion in 1994, 42 per cent of which flow to the new Länder. Including regional, local, ERP, and EC subsidies and financial assistance, the total amount is DM 114 billion in 1993, up from DM 79 billion in 1990.

September

The Bundesbank lowers the Lombard rate from 7¾ to 7¼ per cent and the discount rate from 6¾ to 6¼ per cent.

October

The Bundesbank reduces the Lombard rate from 7¼ to 6¾ per cent and the discount rate from 6¼ to 5¾ per cent.

The Federal Constitutional Court decides that the Maastricht Treaty is compatible with the German Basic Law. The treaty comes into force on 1 November 1993.

December

In the fourth quarter of 1993, the money stock (M3) exceeds its pre-year level by 7.4 per cent, compared with the target range of 4½ to 6½ per cent. For 1994, the Bundesbank announces a slightly lower target range of 4 to 6 per cent.

The 1994 federal budget and a retrenchment package – estimated to amount to nearly DM 26 billion – are approved. With an expenditure volume of DM 480 billion, the deficit is held approximately to the 1993 level, to just under DM 70 billion.

1994

January

The second stage of the European Economic and Monetary Union commences. In keeping with the regulations of the Maastricht Treaty, cash advances by the Bundesbank to the public sector are now prohibited. At the same time, the Bundesbank effectively releases the central and regional public authorities from their deposit requirements (section 17 of the Bundesbank Act) of liquid funds.

Various financial policy measures come into force:

- unemployment and related benefits are cut; the mineral oil tax is increased (Retrenchment, Consolidation and Growth Programme);
- tax concessions granted on owner-occupied old buildings are reduced (Federal Consolidation Programme);
- the corporation tax is reformed (Standortsicherungsgesetz);

– the reform of the railways comes into force with the establishment of the "Deutsche Bahn AG". A new subsidiary budget, the Federal Railways Fund, assumes the debts incurred by the railways of about DM 66 billion.

The contribution rate to the pension insurance funds is raised from 17.5 to 19.2 per cent.

A pilot agreement in the 1994 wage round provides for a 2 per cent pay rise in the western German chemical industry – after three initial "zero-months". The annual Christmas bonus (Weihnachtsgeld) is kept at the level of the previous year. Newly-hired employees may be paid up to 7.5 per cent (up to 10 per cent for long-term unemployed) below normal wage rates. Weekly working hours can be varied between 35 and 40 hours without extra compensation in wages.

February

The Bundesbank lowers the discount rate from $5\frac{3}{4}$ to $5\frac{1}{4}$ per cent.

March

As of 1 March 1994 progressive reserve requirements for sight deposits of residents (6.6 per cent, 9.9 per cent and 12.1 per cent, depending on deposit size) are abolished, and the reserve ratio for sight deposits of both residents and non-residents is lowered to a uniform 5 per cent.

The wage agreements in the western German metal and engineering industry and the public sector mirror the settlement in the chemical industry as they also provide for 2 per cent increases in wages and salaries – including initial "zero-months" (5 in metal industry and 6 to 8, depending on the level of income, in the public sector). With some yearly bonuses (Urlaubsgeld, Weihnachtsgeld) being frozen and the flexibility of weekly working hours – without compensation in wages – increased, the negotiated wage level in the metal industry will rise only slightly this year.

April

The Bundesbank reduces the Lombard rate from $6\frac{3}{4}$ to $6\frac{1}{2}$ per cent and the discount rate from $5\frac{1}{4}$ to 5 per cent.

The law on a statutory long-term care insurance (Pflegeversicherung) passes the Mediation Committee of Bundestag and Bundesrat. As of January 1995, contribution payments, amounting to 1 per cent of gross wages, either will be shared between employers and employees, if agreement on abolishing one public holiday is achieved, or the employees will have to pay the whole contribution. Payments or non-cash benefits will start as of April 1995 for people being cared for at home. As of July 1996, the insurance will also pay for care costs in nursing homes (up to a limit of DM 2 800, in exceptional cases DM 3 300); the contribution rate will then increase to 1.7 per cent in total (0.85 per cent each for employers and employees). A possible further compensation for enterprises has not yet been decided.

May

The Bundesbank lowers the Lombard rate from 6½ to 6 per cent and the discount rate from 5 to 4½ per cent.

STATISTICAL ANNEX

Table A. **Selected background statistics**[1]

	1984	1985	1986	1987	1988	1989	1990	1991	1992	1993
A. Percentage change from previous year at constant prices										
Private consumption	1.6	1.5	3.4	3.3	2.7	2.7	5.4	3.6	2.3	0.1
Gross fixed investment	0.3	0.0	3.6	2.1	4.6	6.5	8.7	6.5	4.2	-3.3
Construction	1.1	-5.8	3.1	0.0	3.1	4.4	4.9	4.1	9.5	3.1
Public	-2.0	0.6	8.2	0.0	0.3	4.1	1.6	1.9	8.9	-0.9
Residential	2.0	-10.0	-0.6	-1.2	3.7	4.9	7.8	4.2	9.9	6.9
Business	-0.1	5.5	4.6	4.0	5.9	7.6	10.3	8.2	9.3	-0.3
Machinery and equipment	-0.9	9.0	4.2	4.9	6.6	8.9	13.1	9.1	-1.9	-11.4
GDP at market prices	2.8	1.9	2.2	1.4	3.7	3.4	5.1	3.7	2.1	-1.2
GDP implicit price deflator	2.1	2.1	3.2	1.9	1.5	2.4	3.1	3.9	5.3	3.9
Industrial production	2.9	4.6	2.6	0.3	3.9	5.2	5.5	3.0	-2.0	-7.7
Employment	0.2	0.7	1.4	0.7	0.8	1.5	3.0	2.6	-1.8	-2.0
Compensation of employees (current prices)	3.7	3.9	5.2	4.2	4.0	4.5	7.8	8.0	7.6	2.2
Productivity (GDP/employment)	2.6	1.1	0.8	0.7	2.9	1.9	2.0	1.1	3.9	0.8
Unit labour costs (compensation of employees/GDP)	0.8	1.8	2.8	2.7	0.2	0.8	2.0	3.3	5.4	3.5
B. Percentage ratios										
Gross fixed investment										
As a per cent of GDP at constant prices	19.9	19.5	19.8	19.9	20.1	20.7	21.4	23.2	23.6	23.1
Stockbuilding										
As a per cent of GDP at constant prices	0.4	0.1	0.1	0.1	0.6	0.8	0.3	-0.2	-0.1	-0.7
Foreign balance										
As a per cent of GDP at constant prices	2.6	3.5	2.4	1.3	1.5	2.0	2.2	-0.2	-0.7	-0.5
Compensation of employees										
As a per cent of GDP at current prices	56.4	56.3	56.1	56.5	55.8	54.9	54.3	54.0	57.2	56.9
Direct taxes										
As a per cent of household income	12.1	12.5	12.2	12.3	12.0	12.6	11.1	11.8	11.8	12.0
Household saving										
As a per cent of disposable income	11.4	11.4	12.3	12.6	12.8	12.4	13.9	12.8	12.9	12.2
Unemployment										
As a per cent of civilian labour force	7.9	8.0	7.7	7.6	7.6	6.9	6.2	6.7	7.7	8.9
C. Other indicator										
Current balance (billion $)	10.0	16.1	39.2	45.9	50.8	57.5	47.4	-19.4	-22.1	-21.4

1. All Germany in 1992.
Source: Statistisches Bundesamt, *Volkswirtschaftliche Gesamtrechnungen*, Reihe 1; Deutsche Bundesbank, *Statistische Beihefte zu den Monatsberichten*, Reihe 4.

Table B. Gross domestic product by origin[1]
DM billion

	1985	1986	1987	1988	1989	1990	1991	1992	1993
Current prices									
Agriculture, forestry, fishing	31.92	34.00	30.24	33.72	37.21	37.18	36.30	36.56	32.97
Mining and quarrying, energy	66.53	65.91	68.67	67.84	69.30	70.17			
Manufacturing	578.85	620.44	624.69	652.67	686.01	741.03	1 075.09	1 126.89	1 096.60
Construction	94.81	100.13	101.68	106.25	114.66	127.54			
Trade, transport, communications	261.46	269.58	279.54	294.66	311.25	346.56	406.18	416.76	419.79
Government[3]	207.26	217.12	225.82	231.86	238.64	253.20	382.02	418.24	439.68
Non-profit organisations, households	42.68	46.42	49.28	51.67	53.92	58.30			
Other services	539.67	571.69	610.56	657.31	713.45	791.22	916.28	1 029.17	1 118.46
Gross domestic product at market prices	1 823.18	1 925.29	1 990.48	2 095.98	2 224.44	2 425.20	2 815.87	3 027.62	3 107.50
Constant prices[2]									
Agriculture, forestry, fishing	31.89	35.22	32.09	34.48	34.97	36.54	36.30	39.34	40.02
Mining and quarrying, energy	64.77	64.09	66.99	66.68	69.51	69.37			
Manufacturing	694.35	690.44	677.00	698.64	722.60	762.21	1 075.09	1 081.25	1 027.43
Construction	124.92	126.77	124.56	127.11	132.46	136.79			
Trade, transport, communications	289.70	293.45	301.19	315.82	330.00	355.71	406.18	405.44	402.15
Government[3]	252.23	255.67	258.96	261.70	262.62	266.91	382.02	388.61	392.88
Non-profit organisations, households	51.93	54.14	55.79	57.47	59.12	61.57	916.28	959.77	976.02
Other services	626.21	666.32	701.82	739.10	773.12	831.3			
Gross domestic product at market prices	2 136.00	2 186.10	2 218.40	2 301.00	2 384.40	2 520.40	2 815.87	2 874.41	2 838.50

1. Prior to 1991, western Germany.
2. 1991 prices.
3. Central and local government, municipalities and social security.
Source: Statistisches Bundesamt, *Volkswirtschaftliche Gesamtrechnungen*, Fachserie 18, Reihe 1.

150

Table C. **Gross domestic product by demand components**[1]

DM billion

	1985	1986	1987	1988	1989	1990	1991	1992	1993
Current prices									
Private consumption	1 036.5	1 066.4	1 108.0	1 153.7	1 221.0	1 321.2	1 607.7	1 722.1	1 792.7
Public consumption	365.7	382.6	397.3	412.4	418.8	444.4	552.1	606.4	622.6
Gross fixed investment	355.8	373.5	385.8	409.9	448.5	506.8	652.1	709.2	705.9
Machinery and equipment	153.0	160.9	169.4	182.5	203.5	234.0	304.7	304.6	271.5
Public	6.0	6.5	7.1	7.2	8.1	8.9	12.8	13.3	12.1
Private	147.1	154.3	162.3	175.3	195.4	225.1	291.9	291.3	259.4
Construction	202.8	212.6	216.4	227.4	245.1	272.8	347.4	404.6	434.4
Public	37.0	40.8	40.9	41.7	44.3	47.1	61.7	71.6	73.6
Residential	100.9	101.8	102.6	108.6	117.9	135.0	167.1	195.4	219.1
Other private	65.0	70.0	72.9	77.1	82.8	90.7	118.6	137.6	141.7
Stockbuilding	1.3	2.9	-0.6	10.3	16.0	3.1	6.7	-7.0	-25.9
Total domestic demand	1 759.3	1 825.4	1 890.5	1 986.3	2 104.3	2 275.5	2 818.6	3 030.7	3 095.3
Exports of goods and services	592.7	580.5	576.6	619.8	701.4	777.5	712.3	718.0	654.8
Imports of goods and services	528.9	480.6	476.7	510.1	581.3	635.2	715.0	721.0	642.4
Gross domestic product at market prices	1 823.2	1 925.3	1 990.5	2 096.0	2 224.4	2 417.8	2 815.9	3 027.6	3 107.5
Constant prices[2]									
Private consumption	1 036.5	1 072.0	1 106.9	1 137.0	1 167.4	1 230.7	1 607.7	1 644.6	1 647.0
Public consumption	365.7	375.0	380.9	389.1	382.7	391.8	552.1	573.0	569.2
Gross fixed investment	355.8	368.5	376.2	393.7	419.1	455.5	652.1	679.5	656.9
Machinery and equipment	153.0	159.5	167.3	178.3	194.2	219.7	304.7	298.9	264.7
Public	6.0	6.5	7.0	7.0	7.6	8.4	12.8	13.0	11.6
Private	147.1	153.0	160.3	171.3	186.6	211.3	291.9	285.9	253.1
Construction	202.8	209.0	209.0	215.4	224.9	235.8	347.4	380.6	392.2
Public	37.0	39.9	39.4	39.6	40.8	40.8	61.7	67.3	66.6
Residential	100.9	100.3	99.0	102.7	107.7	116.2	167.1	183.7	196.3
Other private	65.0	68.8	70.5	73.1	76.3	78.8	118.6	129.6	129.3
Stockbuilding	1.3	2.7	1.0	12.0	17.0	5.8	6.7	-2.4	-20.2
Total domestic demand	1 759.3	1 818.2	1 865.0	1 931.8	1 986.1	2 083.7	2 818.6	2 894.7	2 852.9
Exports of goods and services	592.7	589.1	591.6	623.9	687.0	758.6	712.3	713.3	645.6
Imports of goods and services	528.9	543.5	566.3	595.2	645.8	711.7	715.0	733.6	660.1
Gross domestic product at market prices	1 823.2	1 863.8	1 890.3	1 960.5	2 027.3	2 130.5	2 815.9	2 874.4	2 838.5

1. Prior to 1991 western Germany; 1991 prices for all Germany.
2. 1985 prices for western Germany, *Volkswirtschaftliche Gesamtrechnungen*, Fachserie 18, Reihe 1.
Source: Statistisches Bundesamt, *Volkswirtschaftliche Gesamtrechnungen*, Fachserie 18, Reihe 1.

Table D. Distribution of national income in western Germany

DM billion, current prices

	1983	1984	1985	1986	1987	1988	1989	1990	1991	1992	1993
Compensation of employees	953.44	988.33	1 026.41	1 079.49	1 124.70	1 169.38	1 221.89	1 317.10	1 423.01	1 508.39	1 527.79
less:											
Employers' social security contributions	176.02	185.40	192.63	202.86	211.89	220.51	229.08	247.45	267.48	282.84	291.42
Employees' social security contributions	105.49	111.08	117.29	124.22	129.33	135.60	142.07	152.36	168.30	179.08	185.52
Wage tax	127.35	135.45	145.52	150.01	162.36	165.48	179.17	173.74	207.34	230.16	227.37
Net wages and salaries[1]	544.58	556.40	570.97	602.40	621.12	647.79	671.57	743.55	779.89	816.31	823.48
Income from property and entrepreneurship	324.66	358.80	380.36	418.06	425.30	466.16	516.21	574.70	606.62	613.93	580.21
less:											
Direct taxes on business and property income	59.06	62.62	71.24	73.56	69.30	75.86	89.91	80.92	91.99	94.25	90.85
Net income from property and entrepreneurship	265.60	296.18	309.12	344.50	356.00	390.30	426.30	493.78	514.63	519.68	489.36
of which:											
Retained profits	10.18	3.01	-2.38	33.22	35.64	64.80	54.88	76.19	43.17	27	-9.03
Accruing to Government	-19.36	-20.71	-20.53	-23.30	-30.74	-39.92	-29.01	-29.08	-38.76	-36.56	-45.47
Distributed to households	274.78	313.88	332.03	334.58	351.10	365.42	400.43	446.67	510.22	529.24	543.86
Gross national income	1 278.10	1 347.13	1 406.77	1 497.55	1 550.00	1 635.54	1 738.10	1 891.80	2 029.63	2 122.32	2 108.00
Memorandum items:											
Household disposable income	1 076.67	1 129.84	1 170.11	1 215.70	1 267.58	1 323.15	1 394.27	1 530.69	1 650.47	1 732.27	1 778.61
Household saving ratio[2]	10.9	11.4	11.4	12.3	12.6	12.8	12.4	13.9	13.4	12.8	12.3

1. Including voluntary fringe benefits.
2. Per cent of household disposable income.
Source: Statistisches Bundesamt, *Volkswirtschaftliche Gesamtrechnungen*, Fachserie 18, Reihe 1.

Table E. **Receipts and expenditure of general government: national accounts basis**[1]

DM billion, current prices

	1984	1985	1986	1987	1988	1989	1990	1991	1992	1993
Current receipts										
Income from property and entrepreneurship	32.01	34.74	33.88	27.04	19.89	31.45	34.27	38.57	50.68	49.48
Indirect taxes	226.13	230.31	236.17	245.50	257.11	278.33	302.22	359.65	390.41	408.27
Direct taxes	211.67	228.20	235.07	243.93	255.41	281.76	271.00	330.79	364.95	362.95
Social security contributions	303.98	319.47	336.76	349.87	366.52	383.15	410.46	512.99	560.90	594.74
Other current transfers received	22.56	22.67	25.46	24.96	25.53	24.89	26.05	32.47	38.61	37.17
Total current receipts	796.35	835.39	867.34	891.30	924.46	999.58	1 044.00	1 274.47	1 405.55	1 452.61
Current expenditure										
Final consumption expenditure	350.43	365.71	382.54	397.27	412.38	418.82	444.07	552.11	606.40	622.57
Wages and salaries	187.01	193.88	203.30	211.50	216.92	222.84	236.29	293.60	320.43	335.72
Goods and services	163.42	171.83	179.25	185.77	195.46	195.99	207.78	258.51	285.97	286.85
Subsidies	36.33	37.94	41.31	44.80	47.74	46.78	48.83	69.34	63.99	63.31
Debt-interest payments	52.72	55.27	57.18	57.78	59.81	60.46	63.35	77.56	101.07	104.20
Current transfers paid	334.64	342.03	353.81	371.42	392.53	409.62	472.90	556.51	603.66	657.98
Total current expenditure	774.12	800.95	834.84	871.27	912.46	935.68	1 029.15	1 256.51	1 375.12	1 448.06
Savings	22.23	34.44	32.50	20.03	12.00	63.90	14.85	17.96	30.43	4.55
Depreciation	12.68	13.12	13.57	14.07	14.69	15.55	16.66	20.92	22.43	23.86
Net capital transfers received	−26.69	−25.72	−24.13	−23.97	−23.02	−24.33	−25.72	−55.29	−46.44	−44.61
Gross fixed investment	42.16	42.91	47.29	47.99	48.91	52.37	55.53	74.49	84.89	85.60
Financial balance (net lending)	−33.94	−21.07	−25.35	−37.86	−45.24	2.75	−49.74	−90.90	−78.47	−101.80
As a per cent of GDP	−1.9	−1.1	−1.3	−1.9	−2.2	0.1	−2.1	−3.2	−2.6	−3.3

1. From 1991 all Germany.

Source: Statistisches Bundesamt, *Volkswirtschaftliche Gesamtrechnungen*, Fachserie 18, Reihe 1.

Table F. **Balance of payments**[1]

DM billion

	1984	1985	1986	1987	1988	1989	1990	1991	1992	1993
A. Current account										
1. Foreign trade, net	54.0	73.4	112.6	117.7	128.0	134.6	105.4	21.9	33.7	59.8
Exports (fob)	488.2	537.2	526.4	527.4	567.7	641.0	662.0	665.8	671.2	603.5
Imports (cif)	434.3	463.8	413.7	409.6	439.6	506.5	556.7	643.9	637.6	543.7
2. Supplementary trade items	-1.1	-1.3	-1.5	-1.1	1.1	-1.3	-0.6	2.6	1.2	-2.3
Balance of trade	52.9	72.0	111.2	116.6	129.2	133.3	104.8	24.5	34.9	57.5
3. Services, net	4.7	5.4	1.7	-5.0	-8.4	8.5	8.2	1.6	-24.3	-44.0
Receipts	135.4	144.3	143.6	146.6	154.7	190.4	215.0	236.9	244.3	249.0
Expenditure	130.6	138.9	141.9	151.6	163.1	181.9	206.7	235.3	268.6	293.0
4. Transfer payments, net	-29.7	-29.1	-27.1	-29.1	-31.8	-33.7	-36.7	-59.2	-49.9	-49.5
of which:										
Remittances of foreign workers	-9.0	-8.0	-7.5	-7.4	-7.5	-7.5	-7.5	-7.1	-6.8	-6.9
Transfers to the European Community, net	-7.3	-8.3	-8.2	-10.4	-12.3	-12.8	-11.1	-18.3	-22.3	-21.9
Balance on current account	27.9	48.3	85.8	82.5	88.9	108.1	76.4	-33.1	-39.4	-35.8
B. Capital account										
1. Long-term capital transactions										
German investment abroad (increase: -)	-45.0	-61.7	-55.4	-62.2	-98.0	-95.0	-107.2	-94.3	-113.7	-90.9
Direct investment	-12.5	-14.1	-20.9	-16.4	-20.1	-27.4	-37.4	-37.1	-28.1	-22.0
Foreign securities	-15.7	-31.5	-21.3	-24.5	-72.6	-50.2	-23.4	-26.5	-68.0	-33.2
Advances and loans to non-residents	-14.2	-13.1	-10.3	-18.6	-2.5	-14.2	-43.1	-26.2	-13.2	-30.9
Other	-2.6	-3.0	-3.0	-2.7	-2.8	-3.3	-3.3	-4.5	-4.3	-4.9
Foreign investment in Germany (increase: +)	25.2	48.8	88.9	40.2	11.2	72.8	41.2	69.0	160.3	289.0
Direct investment	1.6	1.7	2.6	3.4	2.1	13.4	3.8	6.2	6.0	0.0
Domestic securities	17.4	38.3	74.1	33.9	7.6	45.2	17.3	63.9	130.0	243.0
Advances and loans to residents	6.2	8.9	12.3	2.9	1.7	14.3	20.5	-1.0	24.6	46.5
Other	-0.0	-0.1	-0.1	-0.1	-0.2	-0.1	-0.4	-0.1	-0.4	-0.4

(net exports: −)

Enterprises and individuals	−16.1	−14.2	−56.7	−11.5	−21.4	−51.6	−19.3	7.5	3.3	−62.4
Financial credits	−7.4	−10.7	−51.5	−13.4	−13.0	−41.3	−17.9	12.3	−23.9	−64.5
Trade credits	−8.7	−3.5	−5.2	1.9	−8.4	−10.3	−1.4	−4.9	27.2	2.0
Official	−1.6	0.1	−0.3	1.0	0.8	−4.6	−5.0	−3.8	−7.3	−2.5
Banks	0.1	−27.7	−59.0	−6.6	−20.2	−56.7	0.6	39.8	64.2	−98.9
Assets	−17.8	−33.4	−65.8	−15.4	−30.1	−81.0	−24.3	19.0	15.5	−120.6
Liabilities	17.8	5.7	6.8	8.9	9.9	24.3	24.9	20.7	48.7	21.7
Balance of short-term capital transactions	−17.7	−41.7	−116.0	−17.0	−40.8	−112.8	−23.7	43.4	60.2	−164.7
Balance on capital account	−37.5	−54.6	−82.6	−39.0	−127.5	−135.1	−89.7	18.0	106.8	34.3
C. Balancing item	6.5	8.1	2.7	−2.2	3.9	8.0	24.3	15.4	1.4	−33.9
D. Change in the net external assets of the Bundesbank (increase: +)	−1.0	−1.3	2.8	31.9	−32.5	−21.6	5.9	0.8	62.4	−34.2

1. From July 1990 including the external transactions of the former German Democratic Republic.
Source: Deutsche Bundesbank, *Statistische Beihefte zum Monatsberichten, Zahlungsbilanzstatistik.*

Table G. **Imports and exports by regions – customs basis** [1]

DM billion

	1983	1984	1985	1986	1987	1988	1989	1990	1991	1992	1993
						Imports, cif					
OECD	298.0	330.2	357.0	331.2	331.9	355.2	408.6	451.7	521.3	516.1	422.5
EC	198.9	217.3	235.7	216.0	215.6	227.4	258.7	286.6	334.9	331.7	252.0
Belgium-Luxembourg	28.1	28.8	29.1	29.3	29.1	31.2	35.0	39.7	45.9	44.8	31.1
France	44.6	45.8	49.3	47.1	47.5	53.1	60.4	65.1	78.9	76.4	61.0
Italy	31.6	34.2	37.2	38.1	39.2	40.2	45.2	51.8	59.7	58.5	44.2
Netherlands	48.1	53.0	58.3	47.8	44.9	45.4	51.9	56.0	62.7	61.2	45.5
United Kingdom	27.1	33.3	37.2	29.8	29.4	30.4	34.7	37.0	42.7	43.6	33.2
Austria	12.6	13.7	15.4	16.4	17.3	18.9	21.0	23.9	26.9	28.0	26.4
Japan	14.8	18.3	20.7	24.0	25.2	28.4	32.1	32.9	39.7	38.0	34.1
Sweden	8.4	9.9	10.9	10.0	10.0	10.7	12.8	13.2	14.5	14.1	12.5
Switzerland	14.0	15.6	17.2	18.5	19.0	19.7	21.2	23.3	25.3	25.4	24.1
United States	27.7	31.1	32.3	26.9	25.6	29.1	38.3	37.0	42.2	42.4	40.1
Other OECD	21.5	24.2	24.9	19.4	19.3	21.1	24.5	34.8	37.7	36.6	33.3
Central and eastern European countries [2]	..	..	..	..	..	..	:	21.8	32.6	35.0	36.0
Non-oil developing countries	42.8	50.4	53.4	48.2	47.1	53.1	60.4	55.5	63.4	58.9	58.2
OPEC	27.3	27.3	27.1	13.2	11.1	10.8	12.4	13.9	14.8	15.3	13.7
Centrally-planned economies [2]	22.2	26.4	26.3	21.2	19.5	20.5	25.1	7.8	11.9	12.2	14.4
Total imports	390.2	434.3	463.8	413.7	409.6	439.6	506.5	550.6	643.9	637.5	544.8
						Exports, fob					
OECD	330.7	383.1	429.3	432.1	439.9	475.2	534.5	544.3	545.6	544.9	467.5
EC	217.7	243.6	267.3	267.5	277.9	308.2	352.7	350.4	360.0	364.7	288.8
Belgium-Luxembourg	31.8	34.0	40.0	37.7	38.8	42.0	46.0	47.8	48.7	49.6	39.8
France	55.6	61.3	64.0	62.3	63.6	71.3	84.3	83.8	87.5	87.0	70.6
Italy	32.1	37.7	41.8	42.9	46.1	51.7	59.8	60.0	61.3	62.4	43.8
Netherlands	37.9	42.1	46.3	45.5	46.1	49.2	54.4	54.3	56.1	55.7	44.4
United Kingdom	35.4	40.6	46.0	44.6	46.6	52.9	59.4	54.8	50.7	52.0	46.6
Austria	22.1	24.3	27.4	28.1	28.4	31.9	35.3	36.8	39.6	39.9	37.3
Japan	5.6	6.9	7.9	8.7	10.5	13.1	15.3	17.4	16.5	14.7	15.8
Sweden	11.3	12.8	14.7	14.7	15.8	16.7	18.4	16.7	15.0	14.6	12.7

Central and eastern European countries[2]	47.4	:	:	:	:	:	:	23.5	37.4	37.3	42.7
Non-oil developing countries	31.6	53.8	54.8	50.5	50.2	52.3	60.9	53.0	57.2	59.7	65.7
OPEC	22.6	27.9	25.2	17.9	14.3	15.5	16.4	18.0	21.3	23.1	18.2
Centrally-planned economies[2]		23.3	27.9	25.9	23.0	24.7	29.3	4.0	4.3	5.9	9.9
Total exports	432.3	488.2	537.2	526.4	527.4	567.7	641.0	642.8	665.8	671.2	604.0

1. From July 1990 including the external transactions of the former German Democratic Republic.
2. Until 1990 central and eastern European countries are included in Centrally-planned economies.
Source: Statistisches Bundesamt, *Wirtschaft und Statistik*; OECD, *Statistics of Foreign Trade*, Series A.

Table H. **Foreign trade by main commodity groups – customs basis**[1]

DM billion

	1982	1983	1984	1985	1986	1987	1988	1989	1990	1991	1992	1993
Imports, cif												
SITC classification												
0. Food and live animals	37.8	38.6	41.9	44.4	42.7	40.1	41.4	43.8	46.4	53.6	54.7	33.4
1. Beverages and tobacco	4.1	4.2	4.1	4.6	4.5	4.5	4.4	4.7	5.4	6.6	6.7	4.1
2. Crude materials, except fuels	26.1	27.1	31.0	31.9	26.5	25.1	28.5	33.5	29.6	28.6	28.5	16.6
3. Mineral fuels, lubricants and related materials	88.4	82.8	88.5	92.2	48.5	39.5	33.6	38.3	46.1	53.6	47.6	33.4
4. Animal and vegetable oils, etc.	1.7	1.9	3.0	2.8	1.5	1.5	1.5	1.7	1.5	1.6	1.7	1.1
5. Chemicals	29.2	31.9	37.0	41.3	38.4	38.5	42.6	47.7	49.7	54.2	54.6	33.9
6. Manufactured goods classified chiefly by material	59.3	63.4	71.3	74.9	73.4	71.6	80.5	94.6	98.4	106.7	106.2	62.6
7. Machinery and transport equipment	76.6	85.1	95.1	105.9	108.9	114.3	128.2	154.4	178.4	226.2	220.6	139.1
8. Miscellaneous manufactured articles	41.3	43.7	49.6	52.9	56.1	61.5	65.7	73.3	83.1	102.7	103.3	69.3
9. Other	9.0	9.2	9.8	10.4	10.8	11.0	13.4	14.6	13.1	11.7	13.8	9.9
0-9. Total imports	373.5	387.9	431.4	461.2	411.3	407.4	439.7	506.6	551.7	645.4	637.8	403.3
Exports, fob												
SITC classification												
0. Food and live animals	19.4	18.9	20.9	21.5	21.7	21.1	23.6	26.0	25.3	29.2	29.6	19.6
1. Beverages and tobacco	2.6	2.8	3.1	3.5	3.4	3.1	3.2	3.6	3.7	4.2	4.7	3.0
2. Crude materials, except fuels	7.6	8.1	9.8	10.7	9.2	9.2	10.6	12.4	11.8	12.5	12.5	7.7
3. Mineral fuels, lubricants and related materials	16.0	14.6	16.1	15.3	8.6	7.1	6.9	7.9	8.3	8.2	8.2	5.4
4. Animal and vegetable oils, etc.	1.7	1.7	2.6	2.8	1.7	1.3	1.6	1.8	1.6	1.5	1.5	1.0
5. Chemicals	51.4	56.8	66.3	71.2	67.7	68.6	76.9	83.1	82.0	84.7	84.7	58.3
6. Manufactured goods classified chiefly by material	80.2	80.2	91.2	100.3	95.1	93.4	102.5	117.2	113.8	113.3	111.0	72.3
7. Machinery and transport equipment	199.5	196.4	218.7	246.6	251.3	254.6	272.8	311.9	319.2	326.2	332.6	214.9
8. Miscellaneous manufactured articles	38.9	40.5	46.4	53.6	55.9	56.8	62.4	69.7	72.3	74.5	75.5	50.0
9. Other	8.1	10.7	11.1	9.7	9.9	10.7	7.0	7.8	8.4	11.6	10.2	5.9
0-9. Total exports	425.4	430.7	486.1	535.3	524.6	526.0	567.7	641.3	646.3	666.2	670.6	438.2

1. From 1991 all Germany, January to September for 1993.
Source: Statistisches Bundesamt, *Außenhandel*, Fachserie 7.

158

Table I. Money and credit[1]
End of period, DM billion

	1983	1984	1985	1986	1987	1988	1989	1990	1991	1992	1993
Consolidated balance sheet of the banking system:											
I. Bank lending to domestic non-banks	1 825.8	1 931.0	2 052.7	2 131.3	2 214.2	2 346.9	2 483.9	2 888.6	3 160.6	3 497.6	3 840.0
Bundesbank	17.3	15.4	12.9	16.8	13.9	14.5	13.9	13.5	13.7	19.3	13.4
Credit institutions	1 808.5	1 915.6	2 039.8	2 114.6	2 200.3	2 332.4	2 470.1	2 875.0	3 147.0	3 478.3	3 826.6
To public sector	427.9	446.8	467.1	471.6	500.5	541.4	547.2	603.6	629.2	739.3	840.5
To private sector	1 380.5	1 468.8	1 572.7	1 643.0	1 699.8	1 790.9	1 922.8	2 271.5	2 517.8	2 739.0	2 986.1
Short-term	318.0	340.2	350.1	342.1	325.8	341.5	375.2	521.0	575.8	571.2	544.2
Medium- and long-term	1 062.5	1 128.6	1 222.6	1 300.9	1 374.0	1 449.5	1 547.6	1 750.5	1 941.9	2 167.8	2 441.8
II. Net foreign assets	119.5	126.3	164.2	227.4	270.8	255.9	288.4	325.4	334.4	338.1	413.9
Bundesbank	66.5	65.3	64.5	67.7	99.8	67.1	45.8	51.8	52.5	114.8	80.3
Credit institutions	52.9	61.0	99.7	159.7	171.1	188.8	242.6	273.6	281.9	223.3	333.5
III. Domestic monetary capital holdings	1 015.9	1 093.0	1 184.2	1 266.0	1 339.5	1 369.6	1 482.9	1 670.9	1 852.8	1 988.5	2 146.0
Time deposits (more than 4-year notification)	265.6	291.9	327.4	362.4	406.2	452.6	491.3	524.9	560.1	564.3	603.5
Public sector	135.4	142.5	150.2	155.2	160.2	165.2	169.3	173.7	185.4	173.3	178.7
Private sector	130.2	149.4	177.2	207.2	246.1	287.5	322.0	351.1	374.7	391.0	424.7
Saving deposits and certificates	659.6	720.6	746.8	781.8	801.5	777.5	835.6	955.7	1 080.8	1 184.7	1 280.4
Share capital and reserves	90.6	98.6	110.0	121.8	131.7	139.4	156.0	190.3	211.9	239.5	262.1
IV. Public sector claims on the Bundesbank	2.2	1.0	2.3	1.1	-4.7	-3.5	6.9	19.1	12.7	0.4	13.5
V. Other items, net	-411.9	-421.0	-453.4	-480.7	-495.2	-533.6	-505.9	-536.3	-544.9	-650.2	-775.2
VI. Money and quasi-money (M2 = I + II – III – IV + V)	515.4	542.3	577.1	610.9	645.6	696.1	776.6	987.6	1 084.5	1 196.5	1 319.2
VII. Time deposits (less than 4-year notification)	219.6	228.1	243.0	252.2	260.5	269.1	325.8	403.3	480.5	527.0	592.9
Money supply (M1 = VI – VII)	295.8	314.2	334.1	358.8	385.2	427.0	450.7	584.3	604.0	669.6	726.3
Sight deposits	199.4	214.4	230.2	246.6	261.1	284.4	303.8	425.8	432.3	469.1	514.3
Currency in circulation	96.4	99.8	103.9	112.2	124.1	142.6	146.9	158.6	171.8	200.5	212.0
Memorandum items:											
Central bank money[2]	148.1	155.2	161.8	167.7	188.7	207.2	216.6	246.1	266.3	305.0	294.3
M3	874.8	916.2	985.5	1 050.7	1 112.4	1 189.6	1 255.6	1 503.0	1 597.7	1 718.7	1 906.6

1. From July 1990 the time series cover the entire Deutsche Mark currency area.
2. Defined as currency in circulation plus minimum reserves on domestic bank liabilities at current reserve ratios. Data reported here are averages of seasonally adjusted daily figures for December.
Source: Deutsche Bundesbank, *Monatsberichte.*

Table J. Population and employment in western Germany

	1983	1984	1985	1986	1987	1988	1989	1990	1991	1992	1993
	Thousands										
Population	61 423	61 175	61 024	61 066	61 077	61 449	62 063	63 253	64 485	65 289	..
Working-age population (15-64 years)	42 390	42 655	42 740	42 798	42 826	42 960	43 258	43 947	44 354	44 890	..
Labour force, total	28 605	28 659	28 897	29 188	29 386	29 608	29 799	30 369	30 682	30 949	30 922
Self-employed	3 054	3 042	3 034	3 050	3 016	3 001	3 011	3 026	3 044	3 055	3 046
Dependent employment, total	23 293	23 351	23 559	23 910	24 141	24 365	24 750	25 460	25 949	26 086	25 606
Nationals	21 584	21 743	21 972	22 310	22 564	22 755	23 072	23 685	24 058	24 056	..
Foreigners	1 709	1 608	1 587	1 600	1 577	1 610	1 678	1 775	1 891	2 030	..
Employment, total	26 347	26 393	26 593	26 960	27 157	27 366	27 761	28 486	28 993	29 141	28 652
	Per cent of civilian employment										
Agriculture, forestry, fishing	4.9	4.7	4.5	4.4	4.2	4.0	3.7	3.5	3.3	3.1	3.0
Industry	41.3	41.0	40.8	40.6	40.3	39.9	39.8	39.7	39.2	38.3	37.3
Commerce and communications	18.7	18.7	18.6	18.5	18.5	18.6	18.6	18.7	19.0	19.2	19.3
Other	35.1	35.6	36.1	36.5	37.0	37.5	37.9	38.1	38.4	39.2	40.4
	Thousands										
Unemployment	2 258	2 266	2 304	2 228	2 229	2 242	2 038	1 883	1 689	1 808	2 270
Short-time workers	675	384	235	197	278	208	108	56	145	283	767
Vacancies	76	88	110	154	171	189	251	314	331	324	243
	Per cent of dependent labour force										
Unemployment	9.1	9.1	9.3	9.0	8.9	8.7	7.9	7.2	6.3	6.6	8.2
Vacancies	0.3	0.4	0.4	0.6	0.7	0.7	1.0	1.2	1.2	1.2	0.9

Source: Statistisches Bundesamt, *Wirtschaft und Statistik* and *Volkswirtschaftliche Gesamtrechnungen*, Fachserie 18, Reihe 1; and OECD, *Labour Force Statistics.*

Table K. **Wages and prices in western Germany**

Indices 1985 = 100

	1983	1984	1985	1986	1987	1988	1989	1990	1991	1992	1993
Wages and productivity, whole economy											
Monthly contractual pay rates	94.7	97.3	100.0	103.5	107.0	110.0	112.9	118.1	125.4	132.6	137.3
Monthly gross wages and salaries per employee	94.3	97.2	100.0	103.6	106.8	110.0	113.3	118.7	125.8	132.7	136.4
Output per employee	96.2	98.7	100.0	100.9	101.7	104.7	106.9	110.0	111.8	112.5	112.2
Unit labour costs[1]	97.5	98.3	100.0	102.8	105.5	105.8	106.7	108.8	112.4	117.3	121.1
Wages and productivity, manufacturing											
Hourly contractual pay rates, blue collar	92.6	95.2	100.0	103.7	108.2	112.4	116.6	121.5	129.5	138.4	145.4
Hourly gross earnings, blue collar	93.6	95.7	100.0	103.5	107.9	112.5	117.2	122.9	130.3	138.0	..
Hours worked, blue collar	99.9	99.2	100.0	100.9	99.4	99.5	101.3	103.0	103.1	100.3	..
Output per man-hour	92.3	95.9	100.0	101.5	103.6	108.0	112.0	116.1	119.9	121.0	..
Unit labour costs	99.2	99.0	100.0	103.8	107.1	106.9	108.0	110.3	115.0	121.5	125.9
Prices											
Agricultural producer prices	105.4	104.1	100.0	94.3	91.7	91.8	99.8	94.7	94.1	91.9	..
Industrial producer prices	94.9	97.6	100.0	97.5	95.1	96.3	99.3	101.0	103.4	104.8	104.8
Costs of dwelling construction	97.1	99.6	100.0	101.4	103.3	105.5	109.4	116.4	124.3	130.9	136.0
GDP deflator	95.8	97.9	100.0	103.2	105.1	106.7	109.3	112.7	117.2	122.3	126.4
Private consumption deflator	95.6	98.0	100.0	99.4	99.9	101.2	104.2	107.0	111.0	115.4	119.3
Consumer prices											
Including food	95.7	98.0	100.0	99.9	100.1	101.4	104.2	107.0	110.7	115.1	119.9
Excluding food	95.0	97.6	100.0	99.7	100.3	101.7	104.6	107.3	111.1	115.8	121.1
Foreign trade prices											
Exports	94.1	97.4	100.0	98.2	97.3	99.3	102.1	102.2	103.5	104.5	104.8
Imports	93.1	98.6	100.0	84.3	79.8	80.8	84.4	82.5	82.8	80.1	78.5

1. Including mining and quarrying.
Source: Statistisches Bundesamt.

Table L. **Structure of output and performance indicators in western Germany**

A. Structure of output (constant prices)

Share of GDP

	1988	1989	1990	1991	1992	1993
Agriculture, hunting, forestry and fishing	1.5	1.5	1.4	1.3	1.4	1.4
Energy, water supply, mining	2.9	2.9	2.8	2.8	2.8	2.7
Manufacturing	30.4	30.3	30.2	30.0	29.1	27.4
Construction	5.5	5.6	5.4	5.4	5.6	5.6
Traded services	26.2	26.3	26.4	26.5	26.5	27.3
Non-traded services	16.5	16.8	17.4	17.9	18.5	19.2
Total traded goods and services	83.0	83.4	83.7	83.8	83.8	83.6
General government non-traded sector	11.4	11.0	10.6	10.3	10.3	10.6

Share of total employment

	1988	1989	1990	1991	1992	1993
Agriculture, hunting, forestry and fishing	4.0	3.7	3.5	3.3	3.1	3.0
Energy, water supply, mining	1.8	1.7	1.6	1.6	1.5	1.5
Manufacturing	31.4	31.4	31.4	31.1	30.3	29.0
Construction	6.6	6.6	6.7	6.7	6.7	6.8
Traded services	21.7	21.7	21.8	22.1	22.3	22.6
Non-traded services	14.6	15.0	15.5	16.0	16.6	17.3
Total traded goods and services	80.1	80.2	80.5	80.7	80.6	80.2
General government non-traded sector	15.6	15.4	15.1	14.7	14.7	14.9

B. Economic performance (constant prices)

Productivity growth

	1988	1989	1990	1991	1992	1993
Agriculture, hunting, forestry and fishing	12.1	6.4	8.0	-4.5	12.3	3.4
Energy, water supply, mining	1.0	6.7	1.1	7.7	2.0	-1.2
Manufacturing	3.4	2.0	2.6	1.9	0.2	-1.5
Construction	2.3	2.9	-0.9	2.0	4.8	-2.3
Traded services	3.1	2.4	2.7	0.5	-0.1	1.6
Non-traded services	3.1	1.7	2.9	1.0	0.0	-0.6
Total traded goods and services	3.5	2.5	2.7	1.6	0.8	-0.0
General government non-traded sector	0.6	-0.3	0.9	1.6	0.7	1.1

Share of total investment

	1988	1989	1990	1991	1992	1993
Agriculture, hunting, forestry and fishing	2.4	2.4	2.4	2.3	2.1	..
Energy, water supply, mining	5.4	4.8	4.3	3.9	4.1	..
Manufacturing	19.1	19.5	20.2	19.8	17.9	..
Construction	1.2	1.4	1.5	1.5	1.6	..
Traded services	40.9	40.5	40.4	40.0	42.3	..
Non-traded services	17.8	18.5	19.4	20.8	20.2	..
Total traded goods and services	86.9	87.2	88.1	88.4	88.2	87.9
General government non-traded sector	11.7	11.4	10.6	10.3	10.6	10.8

C. Others indicators (current prices)

	1983	1984	1985	1986	1987	1988	1989	1990	1991	1992
Total R&D expenditure as % of total GDP	2.5	2.5	2.7	2.7	2.9	2.9	2.9	2.8	2.7	2.6
R&D as % of GDP in business enterprise sector	1.8	..	2.0	2.0	2.1	2.1	2.1	2.0	1.8	1.8
Government-funded R&D as % of total	38.8	37.9	36.7	35.3	34.7	34.2	34.1	34.1	36.5	37.0

Source: Statistisches Bundesamt, *Volkswirtschaftliche Gesamtrechnungen*, Fachserie 18, Reihe 1; OECD, *Main Science and Technology Indicators.*

Table M. Labour market indicators in western Germany

A. TREND

	Peak		Trough		1989	1990	1991	1992	1993
Standardised unemployment rate	1983:	8.0	1980:	3.0	5.6	4.8	4.2	4.6	5.8
Unemployment rate									
Total	1985:	9.3	1979:	3.8	7.9	7.2	6.3	6.6	8.2
Male	1985:	8.6	1979:	2.9	6.9	6.3	5.8	6.2	8.0
Female	1986:	10.6	1980:	5.2	9.4	8.4	7.0	7.2	8.5
Youth [1]	1983:	9.1	1980:	3.2	5.4	5.0	4.5	5.0	6.4
Share of long-term unemployment [2]	1988:	32.6	1980:	12.9	31.4	29.7	28.3	26.6	..
Registered vacancies (thousands)	1991:	331.4	1983:	76.0	251.0	314.0	331.4	324.0	243.0
Length of working week (1985 = 100) [3]	1985:	100.0	1991:	94.5	97.3	95.5	94.5	95.1	..

B. STRUCTURAL AND INSTITUTIONAL FEATURES

	1985	1986	1987	1988	1989	1990	1991	1992	1993
Labour force (% change)	0.8	1.0	0.7	0.8	0.7	2.3	1.8	0.9	–0.1
Participation rate [4]									
Total	67.2	68.2	68.6	68.9	68.9	69.1	69.2	68.9	..
Males	82.3	82.5	82.5	82.2	81.5	80.8	79.8	78.9	..
Females	52.9	53.8	54.5	55.4	56.0	57.0	58.2	58.6	..
Employment/population from 15 to 64 years	61.0	61.8	62.2	62.5	63.0	63.7	64.3	64.0	..
Employers, self-employed and family workers (as % of total)	11.4	11.3	11.1	11.0	10.8	10.6	10.5	10.5	10.6
Wage-earners and salaried employees (as % of total)	88.6	88.7	88.9	89.0	89.2	89.4	89.5	89.5	89.4
Civilian employment by sector (% change)									
Agriculture	–3.4	–1.6	–4.4	–4.2	–4.6	–3.2	–3.1	–4.1	–4.8
Industry	0.0	1.0	–0.2	–0.2	1.2	2.8	1.7	–1.2	–4.7
Services	1.2	0.8	1.1	1.3	1.6	3.0	4.4	1.8	–0.9
of which: General government	1.3	1.6	1.1	0.5	0.6	0.7	0.0	0.8	–0.4
Total	0.7	1.4	0.7	0.8	1.5	3.0	2.6	0.9	–1.6
Civilian employment by sector (as % of total)									
Agriculture	4.5	4.4	4.2	4.0	3.7	3.5	3.3	3.1	3.0
Industry	40.8	40.6	40.3	39.9	39.8	39.7	39.2	38.3	37.3
Services	54.7	55.0	55.5	56.1	56.5	56.8	57.4	58.4	59.7
of which: General government	15.5	15.6	15.6	15.6	15.4	15.1	14.7	14.7	14.9
Short-time workers [5]	0.9	0.7	1.0	0.8	0.4	0.2	0.5	1.0	0.5
Non-wage labour costs [6]	12.8	12.9	12.8	12.9	12.9	12.9	13.4	13.5	13.8

1. 15-19 year old.
2. People looking for a job one year or more as a percentage of total registered unemployment.
3. Hours worked by wage-earners in manufacturing.
4. Labour force as a percentage of population from 15 to 64 years.
5. Short-time workers as percentage of total employment.
6. Employers' social security contributions as a percentage of total wage, total Germany.
Source: Statistisches Bundesamt; Bundesanstalt für Arbeit, *Amtliche Nachrichten*, Jahreszahlen; OECD, *National Accounts, Labour Force Statistics and Main Economic Indicators.*

Table N. **Public sector**[1]

	1988	1989	1990	1991	1992	1993
Budgetary indicators: general government accounts (% of GDP)						
Primary receipts (excluding interest)	44.1	44.9	43.0	45.3	46.4	46.7
Primary expenditure (excluding interest)	43.5	42.1	42.4	44.6	45.4	46.6
Primary budget balance	0.6	2.9	0.6	0.6	1.0	0.1
General government budget balance	−2.1	0.1	−2.0	−3.2	−2.8	−3.3
Structure of expenditure and taxes (% of GDP)						
General government expenditure	47.3	45.8	46.1	49.6	50.1	51.2
Consumption	19.7	18.8	18.6	19.6	20.0	20.0
Subsidies	2.3	2.1	2.0	2.4	2.1	2.0
Investment	2.3	2.4	2.3	2.7	2.8	2.8
General government receipts	45.1	45.9	44.1	46.3	47.5	47.9
Direct taxes	12.2	12.7	11.3	11.7	12.1	11.7
Indirect taxes	12.3	12.5	12.6	12.8	12.9	13.1
Social security contributions	17.5	17.2	17.2	18.2	18.5	19.1
Other indicators[2]						
Income tax as a per cent of total tax	33.5	33.1	31.4	32.9	34.3	33.7
Income tax elasticity	0.4	1.5	−0.3	1.3	2.0	0.1
Tax rates (%)						
Average effective personal income tax rate	17.7	18.4	16.6	16.4	17.5	17.9
Effective social security contribution rate	38.6	38.6	38.4	39.1	39.7	41.3
Standard VAT rate	14.0	14.0	14.0	14.0	14.0	15.0

1. From 1991 all Germany.
2. Households.
Source: OECD, *National Accounts*; Deutsche Bundesbank, *Monatsbericht.*

Table O. **Financial markets**

	1970	1975	1980	1985	1989	1990	1991	1992	1993
Structure of financial flows[1]									
Share of intermediated financing in total financing	81.1	94.5	73.5	75.4	65.5	..	70.4	79.1	..
Financial institutions' share of financial assets	45.2	49.7	44.1	44.2	40.3	..	42.9	45.5	..
Structure of private non-financial sector's portfolio:									
Deposits[2]	73.3	74.7	57.9	60.9	44.7	..	45.4	66.6	..
Bonds and bills	12.0	7.9	14.3	15.0	23.3	..	33.1	17.0	..
Equities	4.8	3.8	4.1	2.8	-1.7	..	3.5	2.4	..
Non-financial corporate financial structure:[3]	100.0	100.0	100.0	100.0	100.0	100.0	100.0	100.0	100.0
Own-financing	56.7	66.4	58.1	67.3	63.5	56.9	57.7	58.8	59.4
Debt and equity	37.0	22.5	35.4	26.8	30.9	29.8	31.4	25.9	27.9
Long-term debt	16.6	18.7	12.9	14.5	13.2	12.3	12.3	18.2	26.7
Equity	2.2	3.1	2.3	2.5	3.3	4.3	2.7	3.9	2.8
Short-term debt	18.2	0.7	20.2	9.8	14.4	13.1	16.3	3.7	-1.6
Other	6.3	11.1	6.5	5.9	5.6	13.3	10.9	15.4	12.7
Internationalisation of markets									
Foreign business of the banking sector:[4]									
Assets	6.5	7.1	7.4	8.8	12.2	11.8	11.5	11.0	12.6
Liabilities	4.1	4.0	6.1	5.7	6.4	6.5	6.4	7.2	7.5
International banking networks:									
Foreign banks in Germany[5]	..	44	88	118	164	177	175	199	228
German bank branches abroad	..	..	..	..	118	128	128	146	159
Share of long-term capital transactions:									
Net purchases of foreign securities by residents	..	..	0.6	30.4	19.1	8.3	25.7	44.8	57.0
Net purchases of domestic securities by non-residents	..	..	14.0	26.5	34.2	10.2	5.4	2.7	3.5
Efficiency of markets									
Divergence between Euro rates and domestic interest rates[6]	-1.0	-0.4	-0.4	-0.1	-0.1	0.0	-0.1	-0.2	-0.2

1. Incomplete owing to lack of information on eastern Germany.
2. National and international means of payments plus other liquid assets.
3. Western Germany.
4. As a percentage of deposit banks' balance sheets.
5. Number of branches and subsidaries.
6. Three-month Euro-DM interest rate minus three-month interbank rate.
Source: Deutsche Bundesbank, *Monatsberichte* and *Statistisches Beiheft zum Monatsbericht*, Zahlungsbilanzstatistik.

BASIC STATISTICS

BASIC STATISTICS:

INTERNATIONAL COMPARISONS

	Units	Reference period [1]	Australia	Aus
Population				
Total	Thousands	1991	17 292	7 82
Inhabitants per sq. km	Number	1991	2	9
Net average annual increase over previous 10 years	%	1991	1.5	0.
Employment				
Total civilian employment (TCE) [2]	Thousands	1991	7 705	3 48
Of which: Agriculture	% of TCE		5.5	7.
Industry	% of TCE		24.2	36.
Services	% of TCE		70.4	55.
Gross domestic product (GDP)				
At current prices and current exchange rates	Bill. US$	1991	297.4	164.
Per capita	US$		17 200	21 04
At current prices using current PPP's [3]	Bill. US$	1991	280	135.
Per capita	US$		16 195	17 32
Average annual volume growth over previous 5 years	%	1991	2.8	3.
Gross fixed capital formation (GFCF)	% of GDP	1991	20.5	25.
Of which: Machinery and equipment	% of GDP		8.8	10.
Residential construction	% of GDP		4.6	4.
Average annual volume growth over previous 5 years	%	1991	0.3	5.
Gross saving ratio [4]	% of GDP	1991	17.2	25.
General government				
Current expenditure on goods and services	% of GDP	1991	18.3	18.
Current disbursements [5]	% of GDP	1991	36.6	45.
Current receipts	% of GDP	1991	33.7	47.
Net official development assistance	% of GDP	1991	0.35	0.3
Indicators of living standards				
Private consumption per capita using current PPP's [3]	US$	1991	9 827	9 59
Passenger cars, per 1 000 inhabitants	Number	1990	430	38.
Telephones, per 1 000 inhabitants	Number	1990	448 (89)	58
Television sets, per 1 000 inhabitants	Number	1989	484	47
Doctors, per 1 000 inhabitants	Number	1991	2	2.
Infant mortality per 1 000 live births	Number	1991	7.1	7.
Wages and prices (average annual increase over previous 5 years)				
Wages (earnings or rates according to availability)	%	1991	5.4	5.
Consumer prices	%	1991	6.7	2.
Foreign trade				
Exports of goods, fob*	Mill. US$	1991	39 764	40 98
As % of GDP	%		13.4	24.
Average annual increase over previous 5 years	%		13.2	12.8
Imports of goods, cif*	Mill. US$	1991	38 844	48 914
As % of GDP	%		13.1	29.7
Average annual increase over previous 5 years	%		10.1	13.7
Total official reserves [6]	Mill. SDR's	1991	11 432	6 59
As ratio of average monthly imports of goods	Ratio		3.5	1.

* At current prices and exchange rates.
1. Unless otherwise stated.
2. According to the definitions used in OECD *Labour Force Statistics*.
3. PPP's = Purchasing Power Parities.
4. Gross saving = Gross national disposable income minus private and government consumption.
5. Current disbursements = Current expenditure on goods and services plus current transfers and payments of property income.
6. Gold included in reserves is valued at 35 SDR's per ounce. End of year.
7. Including Luxembourg.

	Spain	Sweden	Switzerland	Turkey	United Kingdom	United States
	39 025	8 617	6 792	57 693	57 649	252 160
	77	19	165	74	236	27
	0.3	0.3	0.6	2.3	0.2	0.9
	12 608	4 431	3 560	18 171	25 726	116 877
	10.7	3.2	5.5	46.6	2.2	2.9
	33.1	28.2	34.4	20.3	27.8	25.3
	56.3	68.5	60.1	33.1	70	71.8
	527.6	239.3	230.9	108	1 008.4	5 610.8
	13 519	27 774	33 992	1 872	17 492	22 204
	496.2	145.4	148.3	201.1	899.8	5 610.8
	12 714	16 877	21 832	3 486	15 608	22 204
	4.3	1.6	2.2	4.7	2	1.9
	23.9	19.4	25.6	22.8	16.9	15.4
	7.1					
0)	4.7	6.2	16.9[9]	5.8 (87)	3	3.4
	9.9	3.3	4	3.1	2.8	−0.5
	21	16	31.6	21.2	13.5	15
	16.1	27.2	13.9	22.5	21.7	18.2
0)	35.5 (88)	59.8	32.5	..	39.7	36.7
0)	36.3 (88)	60	34.2	..	38.8	32.5
	0.22	0.88	0.37	..	0.32	0.2
	7 935	8 994	12 607	1995	9 912	14 891
	307	418	441	29	361	568
	323	681	905	151	434	509
	389	471	406	174	434	814
	3.9	2.9	3	0.9	1.4	2.3
	7.8	6.1	6.2	56.5	7.4	8.9
	7.6	7.7	..	..	8.6	2.8
	5.9	7.2	3.5	60.3	6.4	4.4
	55 353	57 422	63 893	13 057	184 087	393 812
	10.5	24	27.7	12.1	18.3	7
	17.1	8.1	10.2	12.9	11.5	13.2
.:	87 449	54 659	69 863	22 566	222 522	494 842
	16.6	22.8	30.3	20.9	22.1	8.8
	21.6	8.8	10	13.5	10.7	6
	36 008	12 644	20 541	4 252	25 201	50 791
	4.9	2.8	3.5	2.3	1.4	1.2

	Italy	Japan	Luxembourg	Netherlands	New Zealand	Norway	Portugal
	57 114	123 920	390	15 070	3 406	4 262	9 814
	190	328	150	369	13	13	106
	0.1	0.5	0.6	0.6	0.8	0.4	0
	21 410	63 690	162	6 444	1 451	1 973	4 607
	8.5	6.7	3.7	4.5	10.8	5.9	17.3
	32.3	34.4	31.5	25.5	23.5	23.7	33.9
	59.2	58.9	64.8	69.9	65.7	70.4	48.7
	1 149.9	3 346.4	9.3	289.8	42.2	105.9	68.6
	19 900	27 005	24 186	19 232	12 400	24 853	6 991
	974.6	2 349.2	8.1	248	46.6	71.6	90.1
	16 866	18 957	20 904	16 453	13 675	16 804	9 180
	2.7	4.8	4.3	2.9	–0.2	1.1	4.2
	19.8	31.7	29	20.5	16.4	18.5	26
	9.4	13.1	12.4	10	9.9 (90)	11.7 (87)	7.6
	5.3	5.5	5.5	4.7	4.8 (90)	2.1	4.5
	4.1	8.5	9.9	2.5	–1.3	–6.6	8.7
	18.6	35.1	59.4	24.7	15	23.6	25.4
	17.5	9.2	17.1	14.4	16.6	21.5	17.8
	49.4	25.4	45 (86)	54.8	..	52.9	39.3
	43	34.4	52.9 (86)	54.6	..	55.3	37.6
	0.29	0.33	0.42	0.87	0.24	1.1	0.31
	10 418	10 738	11 973	9 807	8 771	8 558	5 810
	478	282	470	356 (89)	440	378	260
	555	421	413	462	430	502	263
	423	610	252	485	372	423	176
	1.3	1.6	2.1	2.5	1.9	3.1	2.8
	8.3	4.6	9.2	6.5	8.3	7	10.8
	7.1	4.1	..	2.2	5.2	7.6	..
	5.7	1.9	2.3	1.5	7.2	5.5	11.3
	170 258	286 314	8	131 361	9 515	33 808	16 338
	14.8	8.6	..	45.3	22.5	31.9	23.8
	11.6	8.5	..	10.6	10.5	13.1	17.4
	181 925	233 814	..	126 158	9 464	27 164	24 874
	15.8	7	..	43.5	22.4	25.6	36.3
	12.8	13.1	..	10.9	6.8	4.6	22.6
	44 232	55 179	..	12 289	2 902	10 777	10 182
	2.9	2.8	..	1.2	3.7	4.8	4.9

lgium.
residential construction.
on and employment: OECD, *Labour Force Statistics.*
nd general government: OECD, *National Accounts,* Vol. 1 and *OECD Economic Outlook,* Historical Statistics.
ving standards: miscellaneous national publications.
ces: OECD, *Main Economic Indicators.*
OECD, *Monthly Foreign Trade Statistics,* series A.
eserves: IMF, *International Financial Statistics.*

ium	Canada	Denmark	Finland	France	Germany	Greece	Iceland	Ireland
5	27 000	5 154	5 029	57 050	63 889	10 269	258	3 524
8	3	120	15	104	257	78	3	50
2	1	0.1	0.5	0.5	0.4	0.5	1.1	0.2
5	12 340	2 612	2 330	21 782	28 533	3 768	140	1 113
6	4.5	5.7	8.5	5.8	3.4	22.6	10.7	13.8
1	23.2	27.7	29.2	29.5	39.2	27.5	26.4	28.9
3	72.3	66.6	62.3	64.8	57.4	50	62.9	57.2
9	583.7	130.3	121.2	1 195.8	1 587.8	70.2	6.5	43.4
7	21 617	25 277	24 097	20 961	24 852	6 840	25 232	12 324
5	520.6	90.7	77.8	1 035.6	1 257.8	79.4	4.5	40.5
5	19 281	17 603	15 480	18 152	19 687	7 729	17 442	11 480
2	1.9	1.1	1.4	2.7	3.8	1.9	2	5.4
8	20	16.9	22.4	20.9	21.4	18.6	18.9	17.1
4 (90)	6.4	8.5	7.4	9.4	10	7.8	6	7.7
2	6.2	3.2	6.1	5.1	5.7	4.4	4.1	4.1
5	4.2	−2.9	0.1	4.6	5.4	3.5	2.6	3
4	14.4	17.9	14.7	20.7	23.1	15.3	14.4	23.7
7	21.3	25.1	24.4	18.3	17.7	19.9	20	16.3
6	47.9	57.2	46	47	44.2	47.6	32.5	49.9 (8
8	43.1	55.5	42.6	46.5	44.5	37	35.1	43.7 (8
2	0.45	0.92	0.77	0.62	0.43	0.08	0.12	0.17
6	11 634	9 139	8 686	10 928	10 672	5 516	10 731	6 409
7	469	311	386	413	480	169	464	228
6	570	972	530	482	671	458	496	279
7	626	528	488	400	506	195	319	271
6	2.2	2.8	2.5	2.7	3.2	3.4	2.8	1.5
4	6.8	7.5	5.8	7.3	7.1	9	5.5	8.2
5	4.5	5.9	8.3	3.8	4.7	16.9	. .	5.3
5	4.8	3.7	5.2	3.2	2.1	16.7	17.2	3.2
1 7	127 658	34 988	26 508	216 157	409 620	8 014	1 589	23 796
1	21.9	26.9	21.9	18.1	25.8	11.4	24.4	54.8
4	7.9	11.1	7.1	11.7	10.6	8.9	8.1	14
0 7	116 729	31 647	26 953	225 260	344 454	19 831	1 655	20 687
1	20	24.3	22.2	18.8	21.7	28.2	25.4	47.6
2	7.8	7.2	7.2	12.2	15.3	11.9	9	12.4
1 7	12 544	7 445	6 779	25 851	47 729	2 398	307	3 672
9	1.3	2.8	3	1.4	1.7	1.5	2.2	2.1

8.   Included in B
9.   Including non
Sources: Populati
    GDP, GFCF,
    Indicators of
    Wages and pr
    Foreign trade:
    Total official

EMPLOYMENT OPPORTUNITIES

Economics Department, OECD

The Economics Department of the OECD offers challenging and rewarding opportunities to economists interested in applied policy analysis in an international environment. The Department's concerns extend across the entire field of economic policy analysis, both macro-economic and micro-economic. Its main task is to provide, for discussion by committees of senior officials from Member countries, documents and papers dealing with current policy concerns. Within this programme of work, three major responsibilities are:

- to prepare regular surveys of the economies of individual Member countries;
- to issue full twice-yearly reviews of the economic situation and prospects of the OECD countries in the context of world economic trends;
- to analyse specific policy issues in a medium-term context for theOECD as a whole, and to a lesser extent for the non-OECD countries.

The documents prepared for these purposes, together with much of the Department's other economic work, appear in published form in the *OECD Economic Outlook, OECD Economic Surveys, OECD Economic Studies* and the Department's *Working Papers* series.

The Department maintains a world econometric model, INTERLINK, which plays an important role in the preparation of the policy analyses and twice-yearly projections. The availability of extensive cross-country data bases and good computer resources facilitates comparative empirical analysis, much of which is incorporated into the model.

The Department is made up of about 75 professional economists from a variety of backgrounds and Member countries. Most projects are carried out by small teams and last from four to eighteen months. Within the Department, ideas and points of view are widely discussed; there is a lively professional interchange, and all professional staff have the opportunity to contribute actively to the programme of work.

Skills the Economics Department is looking for:

a) Solid competence in using the tools of both micro-economic and macro-economic theory to answer policy questions. Experience indicates that this normally requires the equivalent of a PH.D. in economics or substantial relevant professional experience to compensate for a lower degree.

b) Solid knowledge of economic statistics and quantitative methods; this includes how to identify data, estimate structural relationships, apply basic techniques of time series analysis, and test hypotheses. It is essential to be able to interpret results sensibly in an economic policy context.

c) A keen interest in and knowledge of policy issues, economic developments and their political/social contexts.

d) Interest and experience in analysing questions posed by policy-makers and presenting the results to them effectively and judiciously. Thus, work experience in government agencies or policy research institutions is an advantage.

e) The ability to write clearly, effectively, and to the point. The OECD is a bilingual organisation with French and English as the official languages. Candidates must have excellent knowledge of one of these languages, and some knowledge of the other. Knowledge of other languages might also be an advantage for certain posts.

f) For some posts, expertise in a particular area may be important, but a successful candidate is expected to be able to work on a broader range of topics relevant to the work of the Department. Thus, except in rare cases, the Department does not recruit narrow specialists.

g) The Department works on a tight time schedule and strict deadlines. Moreover, much of the work in the Department is carried out in small groups of economists. Thus, the ability to work with other economists from a variety of cultural and professional backgrounds, to supervise junior staff, and to produce work on time is important.

General Information

The salary for recruits depends on educational and professional background. Positions carry a basic salary from FF 262 512 or FF 323 916 for Administrators (economists) and from FF 375 708 for Principal Administrators (senior economists). This may be supplemented by expatriation and/or family allowances, depending on nationality, residence and family situation. Initial appointments are for a fixed term of two to three years.

Vacancies are open to candidates from OECD Member countries. The Organisation seeks to maintain an appropriate balance between female and male staff and among nationals from Member countries.

For further information on employment opportunities in the Economics Department, contact:

Administrative Unit
Economics Department
OECD
2, rue André-Pascal
75775 PARIS CEDEX 16
FRANCE

Applications citing "ECSUR", together with a detailed *curriculum vitae* in English or French, should be sent to the Head of Personnel at the above address.

MAIN SALES OUTLETS OF OECD PUBLICATIONS
PRINCIPAUX POINTS DE VENTE DES PUBLICATIONS DE L'OCDE

ARGENTINA – ARGENTINE
Carlos Hirsch S.R.L.
Galería Güemes, Florida 165, 4° Piso
1333 Buenos Aires   Tel. (1) 331.1787 y 331.2391
Telefax: (1) 331.1787

AUSTRALIA – AUSTRALIE
D.A. Information Services
648 Whitehorse Road, P.O.B 163
Mitcham, Victoria 3132   Tel. (03) 873.4411
Telefax: (03) 873.5679

AUSTRIA – AUTRICHE
Gerold & Co.
Graben 31
Wien I   Tel. (0222) 533.50.14

BELGIUM – BELGIQUE
Jean De Lannoy
Avenue du Roi 202
B-1060 Bruxelles   Tel. (02) 538.51.69/538.08.41
Telefax: (02) 538.08.41

CANADA
Renouf Publishing Company Ltd.
1294 Algoma Road
Ottawa, ON K1B 3W8   Tel. (613) 741.4333
Telefax: (613) 741.5439
Stores:
61 Sparks Street
Ottawa, ON K1P 5R1   Tel. (613) 238.8985
211 Yonge Street
Toronto, ON M5B 1M4   Tel. (416) 363.3171
Telefax: (416)363.59.63

Les Éditions La Liberté Inc.
3020 Chemin Sainte-Foy
Sainte-Foy, PQ G1X 3V6   Tel. (418) 658.3763
Telefax: (418) 658.3763

Federal Publications Inc.
165 University Avenue, Suite 701
Toronto, ON M5H 3B8   Tel. (416) 860.1611
Telefax: (416) 860.1608

Les Publications Fédérales
1185 Université
Montréal, QC H3B 3A7   Tel. (514) 954.1633
Telefax : (514) 954.1635

CHINA – CHINE
China National Publications Import
Export Corporation (CNPIEC)
16 Gongti E. Road, Chaoyang District
P.O. Box 88 or 50
Beijing 100704 PR   Tel. (01) 506.6688
Telefax: (01) 506.3101

DENMARK – DANEMARK
Munksgaard Book and Subscription Service
35, Nørre Søgade, P.O. Box 2148
DK-1016 København K   Tel. (33) 12.85.70
Telefax: (33) 12.93.87

FINLAND – FINLANDE
Akateeminen Kirjakauppa
Keskuskatu 1, P.O. Box 128
00100 Helsinki

Subscription Services/Agence d'abonnements :
P.O. Box 23
00371 Helsinki   Tel. (358 0) 12141
Telefax: (358 0) 121.4450

FRANCE
OECD/OCDE
Mail Orders/Commandes par correspondance:
2, rue André-Pascal
75775 Paris Cedex 16   Tel. (33-1) 45.24.82.00
Telefax: (33-1) 49.10.42.76
Telex: 640048 OCDE

OECD Bookshop/Librairie de l'OCDE :
33, rue Octave-Feuillet
75016 Paris   Tel. (33-1) 45.24.81.67
(33-1) 45.24.81.81
Documentation Française
29, quai Voltaire
75007 Paris   Tel. 40.15.70.00
Gibert Jeune (Droit-Économie)
6, place Saint-Michel
75006 Paris   Tel. 43.25.91.19
Librairie du Commerce International
10, avenue d'Iéna
75016 Paris   Tel. 40.73.34.60
Librairie Dunod
Université Paris-Dauphine
Place du Maréchal de Lattre de Tassigny
75016 Paris   Tel. (1) 44.05.40.13
Librairie Lavoisier
11, rue Lavoisier
75008 Paris   Tel. 42.65.39.95
Librairie L.G.D.J. - Montchrestien
20, rue Soufflot
75005 Paris   Tel. 46.33.89.85
Librairie des Sciences Politiques
30, rue Saint-Guillaume
75007 Paris   Tel. 45.48.36.02
P.U.F.
49, boulevard Saint-Michel
75005 Paris   Tel. 43.25.83.40
Librairie de l'Université
12a, rue Nazareth
13100 Aix-en-Provence   Tel. (16) 42.26.18.08
Documentation Française
165, rue Garibaldi
69003 Lyon   Tel. (16) 78.63.32.23
Librairie Decitre
29, place Bellecour
69002 Lyon   Tel. (16) 72.40.54.54

GERMANY – ALLEMAGNE
OECD Publications and Information Centre
August-Bebel-Allee 6
D-53175 Bonn   Tel. (0228) 959.120
Telefax: (0228) 959.12.17

GREECE – GRÈCE
Librairie Kauffmann
Mavrokordatou 9
106 78 Athens   Tel. (01) 32.55.321
Telefax: (01) 36.33.967

HONG-KONG
Swindon Book Co. Ltd.
13–15 Lock Road
Kowloon, Hong Kong   Tel. 366.80.31
Telefax: 739.49.75

HUNGARY – HONGRIE
Euro Info Service
Margitsziget, Európa Ház
1138 Budapest   Tel. (1) 111.62.16
Telefax : (1) 111.60.61

ICELAND – ISLANDE
Mál Mog Menning
Laugavegi 18, Pósthólf 392
121 Reykjavik   Tel. 162.35.23

INDIA – INDE
Oxford Book and Stationery Co.
Scindia House
New Delhi 110001   Tel.(11) 331.5896/5308
Telefax: (11) 332.5993
17 Park Street
Calcutta 700016   Tel. 240832

INDONESIA – INDONÉSIE
Pdii-Lipi
P.O. Box 269/JKSMG/88
Jakarta 12790   Tel. 583467
Telex: 62 875

IRELAND – IRLANDE
TDC Publishers – Library Suppliers
12 North Frederick Street
Dublin 1   Tel. (01) 874.48.35
Telefax: (01) 874.84.16

ISRAEL
Praedicta
5 Shatner Street
P.O. Box 34030
Jerusalem 91430   Tel. (2) 52.84.90/1/2
Telefax: (2) 52.84.93

ITALY – ITALIE
Libreria Commissionaria Sansoni
Via Duca di Calabria 1/1
50125 Firenze   Tel. (055) 64.54.15
Telefax: (055) 64.12.57
Via Bartolini 29
20155 Milano   Tel. (02) 36.50.83
Editrice e Libreria Herder
Piazza Montecitorio 120
00186 Roma   Tel. 679.46.28
Telefax: 678.47.51
Libreria Hoepli
Via Hoepli 5
20121 Milano   Tel. (02) 86.54.46
Telefax: (02) 805.28.86
Libreria Scientifica
Dott. Lucio de Biasio 'Aeiou'
Via Coronelli, 6
20146 Milano   Tel. (02) 48.95.45.52
Telefax: (02) 48.95.45.48

JAPAN – JAPON
OECD Publications and Information Centre
Landic Akasaka Building
2-3-4 Akasaka, Minato-ku
Tokyo 107   Tel. (81.3) 3586.2016
Telefax: (81.3) 3584.7929

KOREA – CORÉE
Kyobo Book Centre Co. Ltd.
P.O. Box 1658, Kwang Hwa Moon
Seoul   Tel. 730.78.91
Telefax: 735.00.30

MALAYSIA – MALAISIE
Co-operative Bookshop Ltd.
University of Malaya
P.O. Box 1127, Jalan Pantai Baru
59700 Kuala Lumpur
Malaysia   Tel. 756.5000/756.5425
Telefax: 757.3661

MEXICO – MEXIQUE
Revistas y Periodicos Internacionales S.A. de C.V.
Florencia 57 - 1004
Mexico, D.F. 06600   Tel. 207.81.00
Telefax : 208.39.79

NETHERLANDS – PAYS-BAS
SDU Uitgeverij Plantijnstraat
Externe Fondsen
Postbus 20014
2500 EA's-Gravenhage   Tel. (070) 37.89.880
Voor bestellingen: Telefax: (070) 34.75.778

NEW ZEALAND
NOUVELLE-ZÉLANDE
Legislation Services
P.O. Box 12418
Thorndon, Wellington   Tel. (04) 496.5652
Telefax: (04) 496.5698

PRINTED IN FRANCE

•

OECD PUBLICATIONS
2 rue André-Pascal
75775 PARIS CEDEX 16
No. 47413
(10 94 15 1) ISBN 92-64-14210-X
ISSN 0376-6438

•